NEVER AN ISLAND

PREVIOUS BOOKS BY WARD MCAFEE

California's Railroad Era, 1850-1911 (1973)

Origins of the Mexican War, A Documentary Source Book, 2 vols. (with J.C. Robinson) (1982)

A History of the World's Great Religions (1983)

In Search of Community: A History of California State University, San Bernardino (1990)

Religion, Race, and Reconstruction: The Public School in the Politics of the 1870s (1998)

NEVER AN ISLAND

A HISTORY OF CALIFORNIA

by

Ward M. McAfee

The Borgo Press
An Imprint of Wildside Press

MMVII

WEST COAST STUDIES
ISSN 1041-4037
Number Six

This book and all royalties deriving from its sale are dedicated to the History Club of California State University, San Bernardino. In 1997-98, this club became one of the most active student clubs on campus due to the leadership of its president, Paulla Tilton-Molocznik. It is the author's wish that the club may continue to operate at the high standard set by Mrs. Tilton-Molocznik.

Library of Congress Cataloging in Publication Data:

McAfee, Ward.
    Never an island : a history of California / by Ward M. McAfee.
    p. cm. — (West Coast studies, ISSN 1041-4037 ; no. 6)
    Includes bibliographical references and index.

    1. California—History. I. Title. II. Series.
F861.M158 2007   98-46781
979.4—dc 21   CIP

SECOND EDITION

CONTENTS

Maps, Charts, Photos and Illustrations

PREFACE

Typically, local history starts with the particular—that which is close at hand—and only rarely ties this information to developments outside the local area. At times local history is cast in some region set by academic convention—for example, as in the case of California history, the region of the trans-Mississippi West. In writing this narrative, I have taken another approach. Chapters in this volume regularly concern developments far beyond California's boundaries, and even beyond the confines of the trans-Mississippi West; for California's own history was shaped by events occurring well outside California's conventional limits. This book offers the story of California's past from a perspective that regularly explores concerns far from California in order to explain more meaningfully that which was happening locally. Certainly, in our present, California history divorced from the history of the greater world around it fails to explain local events adequately.

My hope is that readers finishing this book will come away with an understanding of how they relate to California history and how it, in turn, connects with the history of their nation and the wider world beyond. I do not expect this one thin volume to change the essential nature of California history, which is, after all, local history. However, I do hope that it will whet a growing interest in a broader perspective of California's past. I do not pretend that this perspective has been wholly lacking before this volume. Many other scholars have contributed to the insights that I have woven into this broader story. Neither do I claim that this book is a definitive catalog of all possible examples of a broader perspective. The book is simply intended to stimulate a different way to look at California's past. It is not primarily intended for scholars, although I also welcome their reading it. This effort is intended for the general reader. It was written for those who have come from other places and find a provincial focus unsatisfying. It is also written for those native sons and daughters who know little of their state's history and how that relates to the rest of the human story. For all of the various people of the modern state of California, this book is dedicated.

An azimuthal logarithmic projection of the globe, placing California in the center of the world, is presented on the cover of this volume. It is offered for the purpose of recognizing at the outset a danger inherent in a broader perspective of California history. At times, when showing connections with the histories of nation and world, the author may risk suggesting that California is the most important part of either the nation or the world. However, promotion of a "California-centric" view is not what is intended. Rather, I hope to deprovincialize California history by this approach. In modern times, California is clearly not a separate community but rather part of a larger world. The intent of this history is to show that it has long been so.

I wish to thank several people who helped with the production of this book. Kent Schofield, a colleague at California State University, San Bernardino, helped nurture the idea of the project. I also owe a debt of gratitude to Meggan Cote, one of my most creative students, who heard of the work and virtually demanded to read the manuscript as it was being developed. Her many useful comments have helped shape various chapters. Grace Arellano, Bill Attwater, Roxanne Case, Jim Charkins, Celia Corona-Salley, Christian Dietrich, Joshua Hanafin, Lois McAfee, Norman Meek, Deborah O'Hara, Michelle Pla and Paulla Tilton-Molocznik read the manuscript as well and have made helpful comments. Norman Meek also provided assistance in the preparation of a number of maps that appear in the volume. Leslie Anthony proved to be an able research assistant. Finally, Paulla Tilton-Molocznik provided invaluable help in arranging illustrations, maps and charts with the text in the final production process.

Before beginning, the reader deserves an explanation of the book's title, "Never an Island." Early European explorers regularly portrayed California as an island on their maps, mistaking the Gulf of California as extending northward without limit. Centuries later, California developed almost independently, first as a distant outpost in the Spanish empire, then as a virtually independent province of Mexico, and finally as a lone western state in the American Union. Later still, California historians became enamored with Carey McWilliams' description of the region as "an island on the land" and a "great exception" to the rest of the nation. All of these influences contributed to a habit of mind that has come to characterize most treatments of California history. This volume is written to show that California history can be presented in a different way. Its thesis is, plainly stated, that California (despite all of its unique qualities) has never been an island.

I
CALIFORNIA'S INDIANS

Native American cultures that existed in California before the arrival of the white man were incredibly diverse. Every linguistic category known in North America, except that of the Inuit (Eskimo), was present. Scholars have speculated from this rich diversity that almost all of the various groups of prehistoric invaders (coming across from Asia on an ice bridge temporarily linking Alaska with Siberia) worked their way southward, ultimately reaching California. Then as now, California's varied terrain and generally pleasant climate provided a universal lure.

Once in their new environment, they began to develop certain patterns of living that became stable and more or less unchanging (or at least the rate of change was so slow and gradual that it seemed as if culture was a permanent entity). One of these patterns was a lack of complex tribal organization, the Yumas along the Colorado River being a significant exception. Typically among most California Indians, culturally different-but-related tribelets under patriarchs made up each ethnic nationality. While some warfare occurred among these groups, it was less violent and of shorter duration than that typical of more martial tribes in other regions of North America. Given the general mildness of climate, light clothing was the rule. In good weather, men went naked, or with only a loin cloth. Women normally wore only skirts. Both males and females engaged in elaborate body painting. Most of these Native Americans were hunters and gatherers, although agriculture was known among the Cahuilla, Yuma and Paiute Indians of southeastern California. They also enjoyed a relatively dense population, compared to Indians elsewhere. While California's demographic estimates for the pre-European era range between 100,000 and 1,000,000, most modern scholars place the likely number somewhere near 300,000.

While leading relatively simple lives when compared to modern Californians, these Indians were adept at some very complex processes. The close weave and artistry of their basketry is unrivaled anywhere in time. Their sophisticated method of leaching tannic acid from acorns in the preparation of the high caloric mush that constituted a staple of many California Indian groups' diet evidenced that their simplicity was not characterized by simple-mindedness. The irrigation projects of those California Indians engaging in agriculture also revealed a certain technical proficiency.

Their spiritual life has also won the admiration of many modern observers. They lived lightly on the land and in sufficient cooperation with each other to produce a stability completely alien to modern California. Men tended to oversee their sacred stories and rituals. Congregating in sweat lodges, they would pass that which gave meaning to their lives from one generation to another. Men also specialized in doing especially heavy work that called for great strength for relatively brief periods. Women dominated in those labors which made up the bulk of the community's workload.

Mircea Eliade, a mid-twentieth-century scholar who studied primitive peoples worldwide, made some interesting generalizations that fit California's Indians. In a book entitled *Cosmos and History, The Myth of the Eternal Return* (1954), Eliade described how the basic mentality of pre-historic peoples differed from that common to modern civilization. An admirer of the primitive perspective, Eliade held up for us moderns a very unattractive portrait of how we ourselves live. He emphasized that in contrast to primitive peoples (who lived without historical consciousness), we moderns suffer with the "terror of history." We live in constant dread of annihilation, either from nuclear or biological warfare or other disasters; and, Eliade emphasized, the factor that makes these possibilities so frightening is that such real and imagined tragedies contain no supernatural meaning for most of us. Within this modern spiritual void, Eliade warned, many succumb to alcohol or drug addictions or other forms of compulsive, self-destructive behavior.

By contrast, wrote Eliade, primitive people knew no such anomie. Every day, they would repeat the sacred acts of their gods or mythologized ancestors, heroes who set a timeless pattern to be repeated for meaning in existence. The hunt, food preparation, sex, child-rearing practices—all were filled with spiritual meaning for the California Indian. At this point, the reader might protest that spirituality is not necessarily lacking in modern life. This was conceded by Eliade, but he emphasized that the spiritual teachings to be found in Judaism, Christianity, Islam and many other world religions, generally defer questions of ultimate meaning until the end of time. By contrast, California's Indians (who by their own consciousness were not living in a vortex of historical change) found ultimate meaning in the here and now. Their daily rituals provided a link with the eternal.

When they hunted, they became in their own minds the timeless heroes or demigods of their faith. It was the same when they did any sacred act—and most of the significant deeds of their day were sacred acts. They lost themselves in these archetypal activities. They did not try to change their natural surroundings in any thoroughgoing way. They harmonized with them and repeated the eternal patterns of their ancestors.

People living in historical time think differently. Modern people think in terms of "yesterday, today and tomorrow." California's Indians lived only in "today." Their yesterdays were their sacred legends and stories, repeated endlessly in their daily existence. Their tomorrows had no greater goal than to be as today. As primitive people, they lived with no idea of "progress" and historical change. They thought in a fundamentally different way than is characteristic of dynamic modern culture. All deeply spiritual people, even those born into modern civilization, have at least an aspect of this primitive mentality. But California's Indians had far more of this consciousness than do modern people, even those of a spiritual bent.

Anthropologists, such as Eliade, tell us that the elaborate body painting of the California Indians was intended to help them live as supernatural beings, demigods or cultural heroes, whose deeds were full of sacred meaning. Thus adorned, they became in their own minds these archetypal beings, taking on their full grandeur and enjoying their spiritual power. Anthropologists also report that California's Indians were unusually fond of dancing and singing. Their songs and their dances related their stories, the legends of who they were and why they were significant in the cosmos. As such, these activities turned daily occurrences into transcendental events. When they made their baskets or their arrows, they sang and became themselves timeless beings, repeating the eternal ways of their ancestors. When they prepared food, they sang and returned to the solace of that which is unchanging. Throughout every day, they constantly kept in touch with the sacred.

Their cultures were dedicated to preservation of culture. By contrast, an historical mentality is dedicated to the destruction of culture, or put another way, to constant change. History is a story of change, of development, optimally of "progress." Modern peoples celebrate change. To change, to "reform," to find new ways and destroy old ways, is the modern way. It was not the Indian way. California's Indians were dedicated to staying in unchanging sacred pat-

terns of existence. Within these patterns they found their reason for
being.

In contrast to Eliade, some modern scholars who admire the
prehistoric California Indians strive to convince us how much like us
they really were. They praise the Native Californian practices of
burning groundcover to replenish the soil, or their management of
animal and insect populations within their territories, or their practices of pruning trees to maximize yield or carrying on a sophisticated
intertribal exchange system. But, in fact, they were fundamentally
different from us in their world view. They did not think historically.
They did not keep historical records. Keeping track of what they regarded as trivial changes had no value for them. None of the California Indians had any real system of writing to keep records anyway.
They did not live in time, as we do. They were ahistorical.

Usually, to point out that the California Indians had "no history" is regarded as a comment of disrespect. But Eliade's perspective
shows us that this view can be seen as a compliment. He emphasized
that it was this very quality that gave them peace of mind, something
alien in our world of rapid change. To state that they enjoyed mental
and spiritual equanimity does not imply that they did not endure
tragedies or extreme hardships. All people at all times are not im-
mune from these. It does mean that when tragedies befelled them,
they understood why. We might not like the explanations that they
gave to sudden illness carrying away a child or an avalanche wiping
out a group of hunters. We might call their explanations superstitious
and unscientific. The point is that they believed these explanations
that were rooted in their traditions, and their firm belief made them
strong in the face of anything that confronted them.

The modern tendency is not to see the Native Californians as
they were, on their own terms. Even those who are friendly to Native
American cultures subtly want to make them over in our own modern
image and likeness. As we value technology, we want to make them
highly sophisticated and capable of technologies worthy of our admiration. Clearly, they knew nothing of microchips, but they did leach
tannic acid from acorn nuts in a very ingenious way. Other modern
observers who bear a deep prejudice for things "primitive" have described them as "diggers"—hunters and gatherers who rooted in the
earth for the grubs and vegetation that contributed to their diets,
which are unappealing to our modern tastes. Examples of the latter
orientation can be found in the accounts of the earliest European ob-

servers of Native Californians. Pedro Font, a Spanish friar in California during the first years of regular European contact with Native

An Indian Woman Gathering Acorns
Hutching's California Magazine (April 1859)

Californians, described them as filthy and uncivilized. He wrote of the Yumas: "It seems as if they have hanging over them the curse which God put upon Nebuchadnessar, like beasts eating the grass of the fields, and living on herbs and grass seeds, with a little game from deer, hare, ground squirrels, mice, and other vermin." Thus, both friendly and hostile modern observers of Native American cultures essentially have reflected the same tendency—they both have defined them from the values and standards of modern civilization.

Eliade took a radically different approach. He suggested that perhaps the Indians as they existed before the coming of the white man had something of eternal value that white civilization destroyed. "Eternal"—the very use of the word is not in keeping with modern civilization, which has substituted "progress" as a higher value than that which is unchanging.

The most significant aspect of California's Indians was their mentality, which the coming of European historical consciousness damaged seemingly beyond all repair. Many modern descendents of the prehistoric Native Californians now struggle valiantly to recover the richness of the ways of their ancestors, but their yearning is part and parcel of a wider modern angst concerning the loss of the eternal. Obviously, the mentality of modern Native Californians is not essentially primitive. Surrounded by and raised in a general social environment of historical consciousness, modern Native Californians are fundamentally similar to the rest of us. The truly primitive Native Californians are no more.

The last recorded primitive Native Californian was a man by the name of Ishi, who was estimated to have been born in 1861 or 1862. His tribal group was the Yana, and his tribelet called themselves the Yahi. They lived in the western foothills of Mount Lassen, in northern California. The Gold Rush of the 1850s virtually destroyed his people. The survivors of this holocaust hid in the canyons, keeping far away from rapacious whites in order to preserve their ancient way. By the time that Ishi reached his mid-forties, he had become the last of the Yahi. Existing alone, he failed to provide for all of his needs, and one day in 1911, he was captured while lurking around a slaughterhouse near Oroville. Authorities handed him over to anthropologists at the University of California for study. Within a few weeks of arriving in their hands, he experienced his first "common cold." That same winter, Ishi suffered his first bout with pneumonia. By the end of 1914, a persistent hacking cough indicated the onset of tuberculosis. He was given the finest of modern medical treatment at the University of California medical school in San Francisco. At first, it appeared that the disease had been checked, but in March 1916, this "last wild Indian of America" (as he was billed at the time) died.

Even though his mentality seemed to adjust well to the white man's ways during his few years of existence in the modern world, Ishi's body succumbed. This pattern had recurred frequently in the

Americas after the coming of the white men. Scholars speculate that the Indians' millennia of isolation from eastern hemispheric diseases led to their relative lack of immunity to illnesses endemic to that foreign region. Ishi was but one of the last victims of a terrible slaughter by microbes that aided the European conquest and the wreckage of the Native American way.

In 1898, the English novelist/ historian H. G. Wells published a fantastic story of Martians invading the earth, destroying its people and laying waste to the landscape. His *War of the Worlds* bore some similarity to the history of the European invasion of the western hemisphere. In both instances, the natives were outgunned. In both instances, the technology of the invader was superior to that of their victims. But in Wells' story, there was an interesting twist. His pen saw to it that in the Martian invasion, the rapacious outsiders died of diseases native to their victims' homeland. Wells' logic was similar to the actual invasion history of the Americas: One group lacked immunity to the diseases of the other; illness proved to be a more effective conqueror than soldiers armed with the best weapons. But his outcome was different. It is interesting to speculate how modern history might have been different had the European invader not had immunity to the diseases of the hemisphere of his victims, rather than the other way around. Perhaps had history conformed to a story line similar to that of *War of the Worlds*, there might still be Native Californians with the primitive consciousness described by Eliade.

Despite the passing of this consciousness, there are tendencies afoot in the modern world seeking to resurrect it. Modern environmental crises involving industrial pollution have encouraged an idealization of the Native American who lived lightly on the land. Also, the spiritual emptiness characterizing modern civilization has given rise to New Age spirituality which often looks to Native American religious practices for inspiration. Many have romanticized the Indian way in their experimental quests for spiritual fulfillment. Few, if any, of these modern seekers have exchanged the physical comforts of modern life for the actual ways of life practiced by California's pre-Columbian inhabitants. Nevertheless, the homage paid to Indians by many modern people reveals the insightfulness of Eliade's analysis.

Only several of the tribal groupings inhabiting the ancient California landscape have been mentioned in these pages. At the close of this chapter it is perhaps appropriate to at least identify where certain well-known groups predominated. In northern California, the Shasta, Modoc, Yurok and Pomo nationalities were uppermost. In central California, the Paiute, Shoshone and Chumash were prominent. In southern California, the Mojave, Yuma, Cahuilla, Gabrieleno and Serrano constituted major cultures. These no longer preside over the land, as eternal good stewards. The coming of the Europeans shattered their ways of life, leaving their descendents to scour the broken remnants of their lost civilizations for glimpses of the eternal, which their ancestors held so dear.

It is hard to appreciate the fine weave of California Indian basketry from a photograph. These are water baskets photographed in 1890. Courtesy, Huntington Library.

Suggestions for Further Reading

1. Thomas C. Blackburn and Kat Anderson, comps. and eds., *Before the Wilderness: Environmental Management by Native Californians* (1993).

2. Norris Hundley, "California's Original Waterscape, Harmony and Manipulation," *California History*, 66 (March 1987), 2-11.

3. Lowell J. Bean, "Indians of California: Diverse and Complex Peoples," *California History*, 71 (Fall 1992), 302-23.

4. Sherburne F. Cook, *The Population of the California Indians, 1769-1970* (1976).

5. Jack D. Forbes, "The Native American Experience in California History," *California Historical Quarterly*, 50 (Sept.1971), 234-42.

6. Robert F. Heizer and Mary Ann Whipple, eds., *The California Indians: A Source Book* (1971).

7. Albert L. Hurtado, "California Indian Demography, Sherburne F. Cook and the Revision of American History," *Pacific Historical Review*, 58 (August 1989), 323-44.

8. James J. Rawls, *Indians of California: The Changing Image* (1984).

9. Sylvia Brakke Vane, "California Indians, Historians, and Ethnographers," *California History*, 71 (Fall 1992), 324-41.

10. Allan Lonnberg, "The Digger Indian Stereotype in California," *Journal of California and Great Basin Anthropology*, 3 (Winter 1981), 215-23.

11. Jeannine Gendar, *Grass Games and Moon Races: California Indian Games and Toys* (1995).

12. Travis Hudson and Thomas C. Blackburn, *The Material Culture of the Chumash Interaction Sphere* (1983).

13. Rosalind Perry, et al., *California Chumash Indians* (1986).

14. Julian Lang, *Ararapikva, Creation Stories of the People: Traditional Karuk Indian Literature from Northwestern California* (1994).

15. M. Kat Anderson, Michael G. Barbour, and Valerie Whitworth, "A World of Balance and Plenty: Land, Plant, Animals, and Humans in a Pre-European California," *California History*, 76 (Summer and Fall 1997), 12-47.

16. William S. Simmons, "Indian Peoples of California," *California History*, 76 (Summer and Fall 1997), 48-77.

II
CALIFORNIA IN THE RACE FOR EUROPEAN EMPIRE

The official "discovery" of California occurred in 1542, when Juan Rodríquez Cabrillo sailed up its coast. The name of "California" had already been applied to Baja California, and he simply continued the name for Alta (or upper) California. In this way, the region first became known to Europeans, thus beginning the continuous process of change that we call California history.

The name California was lifted from a Portuguese novel familiar to Spanish conquistadors. In that age, the line between fact and fiction was often blurred; and we can surmise that the Spaniards applying the name to the California coast did so because they actually believed they had arrived in a mythical land described in print. The novel *The Deeds of Esplandian*, by one Garcí Ordoñez de Montalvo, described an intercontinental conflict pitting the forces of Christendom against those of Islam. Califía, queen of a mysterious island named California, was allied to the Muslims fighting Esplandían, the champion of Christendom. The novel was equivalent to the Cold War thrillers of our own time, the exception being that this earlier book was possibly considered factually based.

The author described Califía as black, as were also her Californians. Her island was laden with gold and precious metals. The name Califía was an obvious play on the Arab name for the successor of Muhammad. In Islam, the Caliph (or successor) was the highest earthly authority. Having someone named Califía, who was ostensibly allied with Muslims, clearly made artistic sense. At that time, Islam and Christendom were indeed locked in continuous warfare. Constantinople, the capital of the Byzantine empire, had fallen to the Muslim Ottoman Turks only four decades before Columbus set sail in 1492. Four decades after his initial voyage, these same Turks were knocking at the gates of Vienna, from which they were beaten back by determined European resistance. A novel with such a story line made sense in the context of the principal conflicts of the time. Additionally, at that same moment, the Portuguese were exploring down the west coast of Africa steadily advancing their search for an all water route to the Orient. Exotic stories of black amazon warriors, such as Califía, were not uncommon for the Portuguese at that time. The growing familiarity of Portugal with West Africa and the on-going struggle between Islam and Christendom were blended in *The Deeds of Esplandian*.

The Spaniards correlated the dark skin of the natives of Baja California to the residents of the mythical island. The fact that Baja California was originally thought to be an island, not a peninsula, also encouraged the identification. In fact, for centuries afterward, some European map makers continued to portray both Baja and Alta California as part of one tremendous island off the western coast of North America—this long after it had been conclusively proven that California was not an island. Such were the continuing effects of the first assumptions made by the Europeans that named the region.

California's very name was cast in a global context of international intrigue. One can see in the mind the connection between the imperial struggle being fought on the eastern end of the Mediterranean by the Ottomans, as well as the Portuguese reach down the west coast of Africa, and Cabrillo's initial voyage up the coast of the area that is today the state of California. All were mentally interconnected in the choice of a name.

More than even the Christian/Muslim conflict, intra-European rivalries of the time affected California's destiny. Had it not been for Italian city states monopolizing the few overland routes to China still not controlled by the Ottoman Turks, countries such as Portugal and Spain would not have had to search for all-water routes to the Far East. Correspondingly, had Portugal not gotten the jump on Spain in controlling the easiest all-water route down the west coast of Africa, Spain would never have considered Columbus' high risk proposal of sailing directly west in search of an alternate way. Spanish ships that followed the Portuguese down the coast of Africa were sunk by the jealous Portuguese eager to monopolize their new route, just as the Italian city states had monopolized their overland routes that were gradually being cut off by the Ottoman Turks. In the fighting over trade routes to the Orient, Spain reluctantly took the only option left, an option that would accidentally lead to the "discovery" of new continents, Hernando Cortés' conquest of Mexico in 1519-1521 and the Spanish claim to California in 1542.

In this global struggle, all participants were tainted. The Italian city states were selfish. The Ottoman Turks were ruthless. In their turn, the Portuguese were both selfish and ruthless. And when the Spanish regarded themselves as having discovered lands close to the

Indies, they robbed the natives (whom they called Indians) of their
gold and silver, as well as their very lives. The ill-gotten New World
wealth of the Spanish in turn attracted the adventurous English, who
expanded a quarrel with the Spanish royal house over the annulment
of a marriage between England's Henry VIII and a Spanish princess
into on-going English raids against both Spanish treasure ships and
New World communities collecting and transshipping Indian gold
and silver to Europe.

Of all of the English raiders, or "sea dogs" as they called
themselves, Francis Drake was the most renown. In the 1570s, he set
sail from England with a fleet intending to rob the Spanish of wealth
stolen from Native Americans all along the coast of South America.
Sailing down the eastern side of the continent, he progressively lost
ships in his multiple raids. By the time he came around Cape Horn to
the Pacific coast, his fleet had been severely weakened; and when he
reached the western coast of Mexico, only his flagship (the Golden
Hind) remained. Crammed with treasure, it was in no shape to return
the way it had come. And so Drake proceeded northward into California waters hoping to find an easy way to return home.

Passing by San Francisco Bay, which perhaps he did not see
due to fog, it is thought that in 1579 he landed at the bay that now
bears his name (Drake's Bay). He claimed the area for England. His
homeland had violated Spanish claims so frequently that Cabrillo's
earlier paper claim to California was virtually meaningless to him. He
rested there, repaired his vessel and questioned the natives about the
possibility of a northwest passage that might lead him back to England completely avoiding the Spanish enemy. Failing to find the
mythical waterway across the North American continent, he sailed
northwestward, eventually reaching the Far East, from which he continued to sail westward, home to England. Ferdinand Magellan's
Spanish crew had circumnavigated the globe before Drake in the
1520s, but the English sea dog became the first captain to circum-
navigate the globe under his single authority (Magellan had been
killed halfway through his trip, in the Philippines).

Drake left behind a brass plate claiming California (or New
Albion, as he named the area) for England. In 1936, a brass plate with
an inscription claiming "Nova Albion" was found in Marin county,
north of San Francisco. Highly regarded scholars at the University of
California at Berkeley proclaimed it authentic, and for decades it was
proudly displayed at Bancroft Library on the Berkeley campus.

There, it remains. However, in the late 1970s it was proven to be a hoax, as the brass was of a composition and means of production not known in the 16th century. An explanation of the discovery of the plate and its final revelation as a hoax now accompany its display in the library.

Nothing ever came of Drake's claim to California. It was too far away from England and other potential English colonies. In fact, at the time that Drake made the claim, England had no American colonies, except for the pirate coves that provided temporary succor for sea dogs during their raiding expeditions. England was then devoted to robbing Spanish shipping, not setting up its own colonies. Besides, Spain was then too powerful a presence in the New World for England to challenge seriously her claim to any part of Columbus' "discovery." This would change with the failure of the famed great Spanish Armada's attempt to conquer England itself, made within a decade after Drake's return. In 1588, storms and swifter, smaller English vessels attacked the great Armada, which ended in wreckage along Ireland's coastline. Spain continued to be a formidable foe even after this humiliation, but her past aura of invincibility was permanently lost.

Nonetheless, events temporarily worked in Spain's favor. In 1603, England's Queen Elizabeth died; and both England and Spain took advantage of this event to call a truce to their seemingly endless hostility. Regarded by Spain as an illegitimate daughter of the hated Henry VIII, Elizabeth had been forced to war with Spain for her own survival. With her passing, England's new Stuart monarchs made peace. The establishment of England's first successful new world colony at Jamestown, Virginia, in 1607, immediately followed. Peace alone allowed this latter event. Focusing upon new ventures on the eastern shore of North America, the English forgot about distant New Albion.

Up until the death of Elizabeth, Spaniards in New Spain (Mexico) remained fearful of potential British rivalry along California's coastline. In 1602, on the eve of Elizabeth's death, Sebastian Vizcaíno thoroughly explored California's coastline for Spain. His expedition was far grander than Cabrillo's earlier sortie, which had been put together quickly and with little investment. Vizcaíno's mission was years in preparation, and his assignment was to chart the coastline of an area that Spain feared England might take for herself. He reported back that California's Indians provided information indicating the existence of a northwest passage (which Spaniards called the Strait of Anián). He relayed fears that the English already had discovered the location of this secret geographical advantage and recommended that Spain act immediately to create an imperial presence in California and expel the Englishmen imagined to be nearby, supposedly hiding in secret colonies in the strait. Had Elizabeth lived and the English/ Spanish conflict continued, these fears may well have been acted upon. As it was, she died three days after Vizcaíno's return to Mexico.

Peace effectively killed Spanish interest in the area. Thereafter, although periodic official discussions continued regarding following up Vizcaíno's exploration with California settlements, Spain's authorities did nothing. With Elizabeth gone, they just could not seem to generate sufficient interest in the subject. Growing internal conflict within England between the Puritan sect and other versions of English Christianity further persuaded Spain to rest on her weak paper claim to California. Meanwhile, the domestic trouble in England eventually led to revolution, which broke out in the 1640s, resulting in the execution of the British monarch Charles I by the Puritan forces. For the remainder of the century, England was the least stable and most weakened of Spain's potential rivals. As a result, Spain showed virtually no interest in California, which once had keenly occupied Spanish attention. After Vizcaíno's voyage, no ship sailed into Alta California's waters from New Spain for the rest of the century.

By 1700, England had worked through its time of domestic turmoil and was ready to resume its quest for imperial influence. But by then, her principal European challenger was France; and the arena for their competition was control of the eastern half of the North American continent. By then, English interest in California was a distant memory. Although the English/ French rivalry was played out far from the Pacific coast, it eventually came to shape the course of California history.

Throughout the eighteenth century, from its New World base in Quebec, France and her Indian allies attacked New England. At this time, there were some English conflicts with Spain, due to Spain's alliance with France; but English attention was generally focused on French activities. As a result, Spain continued to show no concern with establishing any imperial presence in California. Spain let France bear the brunt of England's renewed national energy.

French settlement of the Mississippi Valley served as a convenient buffer between the English colonies on the North American eastern seaboard and Spain's own colony in New Spain (Mexico). Continuing the pattern established in the 17th century well into the 18th century, no ship from New Spain sailed into Alta California's waters. Temporarily, Spain's paper claim sufficed.

Then, in the middle of the 18th century, geopolitical conditions changed suddenly, pushing Spain to think again of Alta California. In the 1740s, Russia began to move into Alaska. Russian intentions to move southward were clearly perceived, and along the Pacific

North America in 1756

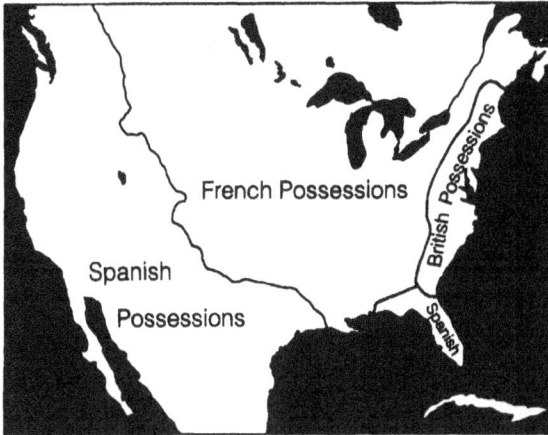

northwest there was no French buffer to shield the claims of New Spain from Russian interlopers. Also, in the middle of the century, the English/ French rivalry came to a climax in the Seven Years War (French and Indian War). In 1763, this generations-long struggle ended in total victory for the English.

France lost both Quebec and the interior Mississippi River Valley. She was expelled from the North American continent. After 1763, nothing separated the victorious English from Spanish unoccupied claims along the Pacific coast. Without its traditional French buffer, Spain finally chose to act in regard to its paper claim to California made by Cabrillo two centuries before. Accordingly, in 1769, the first Spanish settlement in California was established at San Diego. Thus, the Spanish period of California history effectively began.

Spain probably would have substantiated its claim to Alta
California in time, even without the outcome of the Seven Years War.
In the late seventeenth and early eighteenth centuries, both Eusebio
Francisco Kino and Juan María de Salvatierra had extended Spanish
colonies into northern New Spain and Baja California. With these
steps having been taken, Spain was poised for the next logical extension of its empire into Alta California. Had the Seven Years War not
resulted in France's effective expulsion from North America, Spain
might have undertaken an expedition into Alta California in the late
eighteenth century anyway. The fact remains that Spain was not allowed a choice under those more placid imagined circumstances. She
had to deal with the facts of foreign powers threatening her northern-
most claims.

Continental imperial rivalries established the timing of
Spain's actual settlement of California in 1769. Similar to the workings of Nature, the processes of history are interconnected. One example will suffice to demonstrate this truth. The tremendous British
victory in the Seven Years War in 1763 played a role in changing
Spanish expectations regarding California. It enabled José de Gálvez,
the Spanish official pushing most actively for a California colony, to
whip up sufficient support from others. Few Spaniards were blind to
the long term consequences of the loss of the French buffer in the
Mississippi Valley. And so, also motivated by concerns over the Russians in Alaska, Spain moved to occupy California.

The tremendous British victory helped generate yet another
important event—the American Revolution. The expulsion of France
from the North American continent removed the enemy that had kept
Britain's colonists closely tied to the mother country. With the historic French enemy gone, Americans flatly refused to help pay off the
great English war debt built up during the conflict with France. And
they began to consider an idea which had previously been unthink-
able—independence. Six years after the Spanish arrived to settle San
Diego, a new English civil war began in Massachusetts on Lexington
green. The following year, the Americans declared their independence, which they would ultimately win after a long, arduous war in
which they received French assistance. Such are the interconnections
of history.

Concluding her peace with the new United States in 1783,
Great Britain ceded all territory east of the Mississippi River, excepting Canada. Westward moving Anglo-Americans then directly abut-

ted Spanish territory. Shortly thereafter, Napoleon Bonaparte of France muscled Spain to exchange territory due west of the Mississippi River, unsettled by Spaniards but claimed nonetheless, for a small part of the Italian peninsula. Possibilities of a new French buffer loomed. Spain's only stipulation was that Napoleon never sell the area to the United States. Unfortunately for Spain, Napoleon did not keep his word, and quickly sold the Louisiana Purchase to the Americans in order to help defray the costs of a new war against Eng-

Louisiana Purchase of 1803

land. Once again, Spain lost a French buffer protecting her from advancing English-speaking frontiersmen.

Characteristically, the Americans were quick to act. President Thomas Jefferson sent an expedition in 1804-1805 under Meriwether Lewis and William Clark to extend the claim of the vague western boundary of the Louisiana Purchase all the way to the Pacific Ocean. This established an American claim to the Oregon Country. The British likewise had a claim to Oregon established by explorations that had arrived by sea. With these developments, Spanish California was being hemmed in on the north by English-speaking rivals who never seemed to rest.

Thus begins California history. Deriving its very name from an intercontinental rivalry in the eastern hemisphere, California continued to be buffeted by the imperial aspirations of numerous countries in the western hemisphere. Even after Spain finally made its paper claim to the area real by moving in settlers, it was not respected. Russia continued to look upon the province as a future acquisition. England occasionally toyed with the idea of taking California under its own imperial wing, but events would later diminish any serious English interest in California. The new American empire, which appeared to be growing at a geometric rate, was the greatest threat of all. Almost immediately after having arrived along the California coastline, the Spanish settlers encountered ships from New England interested in trade. The American traders took account of the weakness of the Spanish hold on the area. It was a perception that would grow with the passage of decades. A fast clock was ticking for California's Spanish period.

From 1602 to 1769, a period of 167 years, Spain had done nothing to follow up on its claim to California. Its slowness to respond later became significant, when all it had was nascent settlements to face the restless, westward-looking Americans. There is a possible parallel in this story to more modern events. In 1969, the United States landed the first humans on the moon. At the close of the twentieth century, there is little expectation that the United States will soon follow up on its dramatic explorations of the moon a generation ago. The long-term consequences of this inaction will only be known to future generations.

Suggestions for Further Reading

1. James H. Hitchman, *A Maritime History of the Pacific Coast, 1540-1980* (1990).

2. Michael Mathes, "Aprocryphal Tales of the Island of California and the Strait of Anián," *California History*, 62 (Spring 1983), 52-59.

3. Robert Ryal Miller, "Cortés and the First Attempt to Colonize California," *California Historical Quarterly*, 53 (Spring 1974), 5-16.

4. Dora Beale Polk, *The Island of California, A History of the Myth* (1991).

5. Harry Kelsey, *Juan Rodríguez Cabrillo* (1986).

6. W. Michael Mathes, "The Expedition of Juan Rodríquez Cabrillo, 1542-1543: An Historiographical Examination," *Southern California Quarterly*, 76 (Fall 1994), 247-54.

7. John Sugden, *Sir Francis Drake* (1991).

8. Norman J. W. Thrower, ed., *Sir Francis Drake and the Famous Voyage, 1577-1580* (1984).

9. Colin M. MacLachlan, *Spain's Empire in the New World* (1988).

10. W. Michael Mathes, *Vizcaíno and Spanish Expansion in the Pacific Ocean, 1580-1630* (1968).

11. Herbert E. Bolton, *The Spanish Borderlands* (1919/ 1960).

12. Herbert I. Priestly, *José de Gálvez, Visitor-General of New Spain* (1916).

13. Charles E. Chapman, *The Founding of Spanish California* (1916).

14. Iris H. W. Engstrand, "Seekers of the 'Northern Mystery:' European Exploration of California and the Pacific," *California History*, 76 (Summer and Fall 1997), 78-110.

III
SPANISH CALIFORNIA 1769-1822

The Spanish colonizers of 1769 arrived at San Diego both by land and by sea. Each invading group suffered heavy casualties. Scurvy aboard the long sea voyage decimated the sailors. Marginal food supplies weakened those coming overland. Despite these problems, the expedition made progress, established a mission at San Diego and moved northward to take possession of more of California for the Spanish crown. Gaspar de Portolá, who led the military forces, moved overland. Near the end of his northward march, he discovered San Francisco Bay, something that had eluded all seagoing explorers in prior centuries. Apparently, the fog normally surrounding the entrance to the bay had obscured its very existence to Europeans until they encountered it overland.

Junípero Serra led the Franciscan friars who were charged with establishing a series of missions to convert the native population to Christianity. The missions were intended from the outset to be the most important Spanish institutions in the new province. Eventually, 21 missions were built, stretching from San Diego in the south to Solano in the north. Four presidios or forts (at San Francisco, Monterey, Santa Barbara and San Diego) provided necessary military protection. In addition, soldiers were assigned to each mission. Seven pueblos, or towns, completed the Spanish communities settled between 1769 and 1822, when authority was surrendered to an independent Mexican nation. Of the pueblos, San Francisco, San Jose and Los Angeles ultimately became the most significant of the communities established during the Spanish period.

In settling California, Spain's overriding imperial interest was to populate the area with "gente de razon," or people of reason. Spain did not insist that only Spaniards represent her interests in this new land. Anyone with Spanish culture would suffice. Accordingly, Spanish California was multi-ethnic from the outset. Los Angeles was settled with gente de razon (people of Spanish culture) who were primarily of the African race. The soldiers in California themselves reflected the multi-ethnic nature of New Spain. The mission fathers tended to be European. Their cause was to take the local Indian population and make them into native representatives of Spanish culture. This of course included the crucial element of converting them to Catholic Christianity and saving their eternal souls.

While transforming the native population would eventually secure California for the Spanish empire, it was generally acknowledged that this process would take time. The colonial history of Mexico suggested that a decade was needed to work the cultural transformation. However, this would prove to be insufficient in California, where even after 60 years the local Indians were deemed unworthy of "gente de razon" status. At the outset, it was not expected that the California missions would fail in their primary task of imparting Spanish culture to local natives. In any case, until sufficient numbers of gente de razon were on the scene, it was necessary to move citizens up from New Spain to gain a firm foothold. Early experience had shown that large numbers could not come by sea. Spanish ships from the south had to sail against the current, which sweeps down the California coastline and makes northerly movement by sea difficult. The seaborne contingent of the first colonizing expedition into San Diego had been wasted by scurvy suffered on the arduous, time-consuming voyage. It was conceded that settlers would have to come overland.

Juan Bautista de Anza, a military man, was given the job of finding the best overland trail, which he established in 1774. The route led through Yuma Indian country in what is today the southeastern corner of modern California. He plied the natives with gifts and diplomatic charm, and they assisted him in moving over 200 people and a like number of cattle across the Colorado River. The party, never far from water and forage, enjoyed some births along the way and two years later arrived in San Francisco with more people than had begun the journey.

The tremendous success of this experiment encouraged the Spaniards to assume that they had found the means needed to plant a colonial outpost in this northern province. Unfortunately, their attitude was not warranted. The Yumas had sensed that too many of the Spaniards whom they encountered held them in contempt. Too many mission fathers regarded them as lazy, filthy savages, offensive in their very being. Too many soldiers revealed their disregard by trampling willfully through their cornfields. Only the presents brought by the gente de razon greased the uneasy relationship. And then these too were eliminated as an unnecessary expenditure. The result was an Indian revolt in 1781, in which the Yumas killed all the male Spaniards in their area and shut down De Anza's overland trail. From that point forward, the California colony was forced to rely on internal growth and a slow conversion process to increase the numbers of gente de razon in the new land. De Anza had selected the only viable route to move large numbers overland. After it became inoperable, the California colony suffered the chronic disadvantage of being weak and underpopulated in a world where imperial rivals only respected strength.

Given their paucity of numbers, the people of Spanish culture in California developed a unique defense plan that attempted to adjust to their handicap. First, Spanish settlements were limited to coastal areas. Second, very few land grants were bestowed during the period that Spain controlled California, as gifts of land in the interior would only serve to scatter their meager force and leave them vulnerable not only to foreign attacks by sea but to local Indian attacks as well. Hugging the coastline between San Francisco and San Diego, northern California's settlers were instructed to respond to a major attack by taking advantage of the southward moving ocean current and rush all available Spanish forces to southern California for concentrated resistance.

Spanish concern focused on two foreign nations—Russia and the United States. Shortly after achieving its independence in 1783, the United States became a presence in California waters. American merchants were exceptionally entrepreneurial, given the negative impact of national independence upon their past mode of making a living. As long as the Americans had remained in the British empire, they had been allowed to carry British commerce in American ships. With independence, this advantage disappeared. British commerce was reserved for only those ships registered with British citizens. Consequently, the Americans had to scramble for new business opportunities wherever they could find them. Enterprising New Englanders sailed the world wide, looking for trade. In China, they found customers hungry for warm fur garments to endure cold winters. Along the Pacific coast, they found the furs demanded in Asia. California sea otter pelts made especially fine coats. The Russians in Alaska were involved in this same trade but needed food, which the Americans were willing to bring them in exchange for their furs.

All European powers at that time practiced an economic theory known as mercantilism. According to this idea, the wealth of the world was static and the proper goal of each nation was to acquire the largest percentage of it as possible. Accordingly, each nation sought to minimize its business dealings with rival nations, in order to keep its wealth solely within its own empire. Great Britain actively discouraged British merchandise being transported in American ships, as that would transfer British wealth to Americans. Russia felt the same way and did not want to buy food from the Americans, as that would transfer Russian wealth to the Americans. Accordingly, the Russians began to move into California waters with the idea of establishing their own colony that could both trap sea-otter pelts and raise food for their colony in Alaska.

The Russians knew that the Spanish claimed territory as far north as the Oregon country but they also did not respect mere paper claims. Less than 100 miles north of San Francisco Bay, there was no Spanish presence. And there they established Ft. Ross in 1812, with the dual purpose of raising food and trapping furs. Spanish authorities looked at Ft. Ross with a worried eye but could do nothing. Spanish forces in California were too weak to expel the Russians, and the latter knew it. In fact, Spain could not even enforce its mercantilistic laws there. And American ships were ever willing to tempt Russians, Spaniards or anyone else to violate the mercantilistic regulations of their homeland. They appeared off of California's coast with merchandise to trade for food raised at the missions; the Spanish fathers regularly succumbed to the temptation. Ft. Ross never was very successful in raising the foodstuffs, and so the Americans remained in business shipping mission-grown food to Alaska.

From 1796 through 1815, Europe was at war. Napoleon's France exploded outward with a revolutionary fervor that threatened to conquer all of European civilization. The Spanish monarchy was no match for this force and was bullied by the French dictator. In the last chapter, it was shown how Napoleon forced Spain to trade away Louisiana in exchange for a small part of Italy. Monarchical Spain was preoccupied with this French tidal wave, so proper maintenance of its American colonies was neglected. In Spain's California outpost, mission fathers and Spanish soldiers alike were in rags, due to the failure of the mother country to provide essentials during this time of international upheaval. The Americans stepped into the void and provided the goods needed for the California colony to survive. As these were hard times, gente de razon broke the economic rules of their empire. As a consequence, American traders became more familiar

Ft. Ross, as portrayed in Duhaut-Cilly's *Voyage Autour du Monde* (1835)

with California. Their reports sent east whetted still more American interest in the province.

One might speculate whether Spain's control over California might not have lasted longer had Napoleon never arose to demand a world empire for himself. Had the French dictator not weakened Spain at this crucial juncture, its California colony may have been established upon a more solid foundation. But this we cannot know. Unlike a scientific experiment, the conditions of history cannot be slightly altered and repeated to gauge the relative significance of various causal factors of an event. That which is certain is this: Spain was forced to neglect her American possessions during the Napoleonic Wars, and during this time those New World outposts acquired a taste for independence. In California, this fact translated into increasing illegal contacts between American merchants and local California authorities.

After Napoleon was defeated, it was too late for Spain to recover its empire in the western hemisphere. The Wars of Latin American Independence were underway. Not only were gente de razon throughout Latin America encouraged to break away from Spain by the long period of neglect, they also had become inspired by the successful example of the United States that had shown that a former colony could successfully detach from its mother country. In fact, the movements for separation began in many parts of South America even before Napoleon's defeat. In New Spain (Mexico), disturbances also began quite early, but did not result in a declaration of independence until 1821. The new Mexican nation claimed California. It took many months for the news to arrive in the province.

On the European continent, Austrian prince Klemens von Metternich was fashioning a post-Napoleonic order that was fundamentally inharmonious with the kind of American liberalism that had encouraged both French radicalism and Latin American independence. However, Great Britain was most wary of Metternich's master plan, which it feared might lead to a reconquest of Latin America for Spain. English traders had found new markets in Latin American lands, no longer bound by the exclusionary rules of Spanish mercantilism, and wanted no restoration of Spanish authority in those areas. For similar reasons, neither did the United States. Accordingly, the United States and England began to work most closely together for this end, despite the fact that between 1812 and 1815 the two had been involved in a bitter war.

The clever Americans knew that Great Britain, as the possessor of the world's most powerful navy, would never allow a European reconquest of Latin America and the expulsion of British merchants. So on its own, in 1823, the United States issued a statement of national policy that became known as the Monroe Doctrine. President James Monroe warned all European powers against either developing new colonies in the Western Hemisphere or attempting to control those that had been lost due to wars of national independence. Of course, he set no such restrictions upon American behavior. Instead, he implied that the United States would be the protector of the new nations of Latin America.

The Monroe Doctrine also warned the Russians to back away from California. As a claimant to the Oregon country, the United States wanted to set as northerly a boundary between that region and Russian Alaska as they were able. It certainly did not want Russia to establish a presence south of the Oregon country. Monroe let Russia know that under no circumstances would the United States allow Ft. Ross to expand beyond anything other than a miserable, little outpost far from any other Russian settlement. From that point on, Russian expansionism in California ceased. Ft. Ross remained in Russian hands until 1842, but dreams of a Russian empire in California ended with the American challenge. It was not in Russia's imperial interests to risk war with the United States. Besides, increasingly it was clear that California's sea otters were being overtrapped and that they were not an unlimited resource. The Russians could not think of any good reason to stay.

Meanwhile, some gente de razon in California secretly prayed for a Spanish reconquest of their province. California's mission fathers especially were disapproving of Mexico's declaration of independence. Most of them were of Spanish birth, and Mexico's growing anti-clerical attitudes did not encourage their loyalty to the new nation. The Roman Catholic church, a leading conservative force upon the European continent, had never been favored by the forces identified with the American and French Revolutions. Latin America's revolutions were no different. Although the church had a role in Mexico's struggle for independence, a definite anti-clerical spirit moved the liberal forces contending for power in the new nation. Accordingly, California's mission fathers increasingly became an alienated element after 1822. This fact, in turn, motivated Mexican efforts to remove California's most important institution from church control.

Long before Mexican independence, relations between the state and the mission fathers had been strained. Father Serra had complained about Spanish soldiers assigned to his missions. He disliked their worldly attitudes, their air of independence from his authority and their treatment of the Indians in the missions. He complained to his superiors of soldiers raping and otherwise abusing Native Californians. For their part, the military forces assigned to California similarly complained against the mission fathers to their superiors in New Spain. Totally reliant upon the generosity of the mission fathers for supplies produced at the missions, the soldiers sensed the displeasure of these clerics in their short rations. Both groups constantly tattled on each other throughout the Spanish period, so that a mass of evidence exists today concerning the negative side of life within the missions.

Interestingly, this information fueled a controversy two centuries later. In the 1980s, an effort to canonize Junípero Serra as a saint in the Roman Catholic church produced a storm of protest from the descendents of California's Indians. The latter detest Serra as a symbol of a system that worked to destroy their native cultures. Episodes of sadistic mission fathers abusing their authority, incidents that had been trumpeted centuries before by the military critics of the early mission fathers, again were circulated, this time for the consideration of a much wider audience. Church disclaimers followed, as a battle of historical interpretation captured at least part of the public imagination.

The facts are these: The Indians were usually bribed to enter the missions by food and presents. Church doctrine held then, as well as now, that no force was to be used in conversion. However, this rule was violated in colonial California. For example, as soon as the fathers were convinced that a group of Indians had accepted Jesus Christ as their Lord and Savior, these natives were not allowed to leave the missions, except for short visits outside. The truly voluntary aspect of the Christian conversion process, apparent both in a close reading of the New Testament and in the preferences of twentieth-century civilization, was lacking. Throughout the history of Christianity, culture often has shaped the actual practices of the church far more than Biblical teachings. At that time, the spirit of the Inquisition was still alive in Spanish culture. Methods of force to support true religion were countenanced. Mission fathers argued that close supervision was needed to keep the new "converts" from backsliding.

While some mission fathers were kindly, others abused their positions of authority.

Many Indians were short-lived in the missions, dying of the plagues of European diseases such as smallpox that swept through the close quarters of the missions. The friars could clearly see that enclosure in the missions threatened the longevity of their native captives; but they regarded the fate of their eternal souls to be of greater importance than the well being of their physical bodies, and the deaths continued on a genocidal scale. At that time, such practices were common throughout Latin America; and the type of discipline administered by the mission fathers was common in Europe. California's Indians were not being held to an unusual standard; but due to their susceptibility to European diseases, they rapidly perished in captivity. And those that survived remained captives. The early expectation that they would graduate within a decade of training was never fulfilled. The mission fathers justified their disinclination to release their Indian charges out into the wider society by claiming they were not ready for such freedom. The comfortable society created in California's missions for the fathers discouraged a policy of early release which would have disrupted the production of the missions that was already being affected by the factor of frequent disease and premature death.

During the Mexican period, criticism of the mission system increased. The greed of those wanting the mission lands (some of the best arable coastal land in California) fed the controversy. In the end, these critics succeeded. In the 1830s, the missions were disbanded and at least part of the mission lands were distributed to the Indians that had been held captive within them for so long. But quickly, these lands were transferred to large landholders. In the end, the Indians were left with nothing, begging in rags for enough to survive, divorced from their old cultures, yet without an adequate home in their new one, dying in their newfound freedom. Perhaps the mission fathers had been right that the Indians were not ready to compete with the gente de razon in Hispanic culture. In any case, slavery proved a poor teacher of how to survive in freedom.

California's mission system bore bitter fruit. Today, when evangelizing aboriginal peoples, the Roman Catholic church seeks to leave the cultures of those converted as undisturbed as possible. By contrast, the task of Serra and his colleagues was to destroy native cultures and replace them with Spanish ways. The failure of California's Indians to become "gente de razon" showed that this was no easy task. Neither was it a positive effort. California's mission system is an historic example of tragic moral irony.

Suggestions for Further Reading

1. Diane Spencer-Hancock and William E. Pritchard, "El Castillo de Monterey, Frontline of Defense, Uncovering the Spanish Presence in Alta California," *California History*, 63 (Summer 1984), 230-40.

2. Richard S. Whitehead, "Alta California's Four Fortresses," *Southern California Quarterly*, 65 (Spring 1983), 67-94.

3. Harry Kelsey, "A New Look at the Founding of Old Los Angeles," California *Historical Quarterly*, 55 (Winter 1976), 326-39.

4. John Caughey, "The Distant Pawn of Empire," *California History*, 60 (Spring 1981), 6-27.

5. William Harrison Richardson, *Mexico Through Russian Eyes, 1806-1840* (1988).

6. Sister Magdalen Coughlin, CSJ, "Commercial Foundations of Political Interest in the Opening Pacific, 1789-1829," *California Historical Quarterly*, 50 (March 1971), 15-34.

7. Robert H. Jackson and Edward Castillo, *Indians, Franciscans, and Spanish Colonization: The Impact of the Mission System on California Indians* (1995).

8. Robert Archibald, "The Economy of the Alta California Missions, 1803-1821," *Southern California Quarterly*, 58 (Summer 1976), 227-40.

9. Francis F. Guest, "An Examination of the Thesis of S.F. Cook on the Forced Conversion of Indians in the California Missions," *Southern California Quarterly*, 61 (Spring 1979), 1-78.

10. Rupert Costo and Jeanette Henry Costo, *The Missions of California: A Legacy of Genocide* (1987).

11. Francis F. Guest, "An Inquiry into the Role of the Discipline in California Mission Life," *Southern California Quarterly*, 71 (Spring 1989), 1-68.

12. Linda Lyngheim, *The Indians and the California Missions* (1990).

13. Albert L. Hurtado, "Sexuality in California's Franciscan Missions: Cultural Perceptions and Sad Realities," *California History*, 71 (Fall 1992), 370-85.

14. Steven W. Hackel, "Land, Labor, and Production: The Colonial Economy of Spanish and Mexican California," *California History*, 76 (Summer and Fall, 1997), 111-46.

15. Michael J. Gonzales, "'The Child of the Wilderness Weeps for the Father of Our Country:' The Indian and the Politics of Church and State in Provincial California," *California History*, 76 (Summer and Fall, 1997), 147-72.

16. Randall Milliken, *A Time of Little Choice: The Disintegration of Tribal Culture in the San Francisco Bay Area, 1765-1810* (1995).

IV
THE MEXICAN PERIOD 1822-1848

In 1824, major Indian revolts occurred at three missions in the greater Santa Barbara area. Predictably, they were subdued with force, but these events were proof that the captives were not pleased with their circumstances. These uprisings, together with the growing number of gente de razon spreading stories about the multiple injustices occurring behind mission walls, made California's mission system increasingly controversial. In any case, these institutions of forcible confinement had lasted far longer than originally intended. Accordingly, in 1833, Mexico ordered that the missions be "secularized," a term which meant that they were to be systematically dismantled. The process of secularization occurred in stages, affecting only a few missions at a time so as to minimize the impression of a major upheaval. Up until the eve of the war with the United States, some missions remained open. Nonetheless, after 1833, no real investment of either personnel or treasure was made in the missions; and these once grand institutions crumbled into disrepair and ruin.

During the Mexican period, the old Spanish policy of minimizing the number of land grants was discontinued. The reasons were several. First, government both in California and in Mexico City was highly unstable, as power passed from first one group to another. Each faction, during its time of power, bestowed California land grants upon its favorites. Second, with the decline of the sea-otter trade due to overtrapping, cattle ranching came to replace it as the backbone of California's economy. The New England ships still came, but increasingly they traded their bric-a-brac for the hides and tallow of California cattle. The hides were used in making boots and shoes in New England. The tallow was valuable for candles. Cattle were killed for these two products alone--their carcasses left to rot. Given the open-range character of this enterprise, large herds were needed on many ranchos consisting of imperial-size domains. California's original cattle, brought during the brief period before 1781 when the De Anza Trail remained open, had multiplied and often roamed wild and unclaimed. The hide and tallow trade put a premium on branding them for market. Also, land was needed for the new cattle barons to locate their herds. Some of this land was taken from the defunct missions. Other fiefdoms were received directly in the form of Mexican land grants.

One final reason for the multiplication of land grants during the Mexican period was the suspicion in the minds of even the most patriotic Mexicans that California might not long remain in Mexican hands. While an unspeakable thought in many Mexican quarters, the weak hold of the new nation upon California alerted even the dullest observers that it could easily be seized by a foreign enemy or be lost by an internal secessionist movement. This realization grew rapidly in the early 1840s, when Richard Henry Dana's *Two Years Before the Mast* (1840) publicized the wonder of California in the years of the hide and tallow trade. Losing faith in the possibilities of keeping this choice area from the Yankee grasp for long, the number of Mexican land grants grew geometrically as the Mexican War grew closer. The land was certain to be of no value to Mexico and her friends if these grants could not be made in time.

The Americans did not conceal their growing interest in California. American merchants and traders had already come to the province by sea, and they continued coming. But in a few years after the initial proclamation of the Monroe Doctrine, Americans began to arrive overland as well. The first arrivals were Mountain Men, Americans who trapped furs in the Far West and lived in the manner of nomadic Indians. Jedediah Strong Smith arrived in southern California in 1826. He was temporarily imprisoned as an illegal alien but was ultimately released after giving his promise that he would quit California forever.

Smith was unusual in being most articulate for a man who lived by his wits in wild environments, and his stories of California shared at annual assemblies of Mountain Men in the Salt Lake region spurred others to follow. James Ohio Pattie arrived two years after Smith. Like Smith, he was imprisoned and subsequently released. These were just the first of a growing number of American fur-trappers, who were increasingly tolerated as their comings and goings became impossible to regulate. An additional factor encouraged American infiltration. California's Mexicans (or Californios) were not of one mind concerning governmental affairs, and Americans present in the colony found they could maximize their own local privileges by playing one faction off against another.

Johann Sutter, who arrived by sea in 1839, was a German Swiss rather than an American, but he associated with the Americans sensing that they were an important minority and would probably determine California's future. Sutter's dream was to build an empire far from the Mexican settlements in the interior of California. To succeed, he needed the aid not only of Californio leaders but of energetic men familiar with the interior. He purchased cannon and weapons from the Russians, then in the process of dismantling Ft. Ross, and transferred them to his own fort at the confluence of the Sacramento and American rivers. Due to his own successful manipulation of local California officialdom, he acquired a huge land grant in the Sacramento Valley to serve as the basis for his New Helvetian empire. Through his American connections, he sent word for American pioneers to come overland and settle upon his domain. At that time, Americans were leaving regularly from Missouri to the Oregon Country, which was jointly claimed between the United States and Great Britain. Some were persuaded to leave the Oregon Trail and come to California instead. In 1841, the first American agricultural pioneers arrived under the command of John Bidwell. Under Sutter's tutelage, Bidwell too learned how best to ally himself with one local faction against another for his own advantage. Consequently, he too received a large interior land grant. Ironically, some land grants were going to those who would ultimately undermine Mexican authority in the province.

Commodore Thomas ap Catesby Jones, commander of the American Pacific fleet, fully revealed his country's intention to take California. In 1842, while in Peruvian waters, he received a false report that the United States and Mexico were at war. The cause for war supposedly involved many depredations upon American citizens and their property during Mexico's turbulent early years of independence. The American government demanded and had not received satisfaction for these claims. Commodore Jones moved quickly, sailing northward at top speed, and seized Monterey (California's capital) in October 1842. As war in fact had not broken out, he quickly realized his error, apologized and left. But the incident revealed much.

Both Mexico and California were in seemingly constant civil unrest. Spanish culture had conditioned the gente de razon to take orders from established authorities. Then, revolution had suddenly created a new republican form of government with no clear authority other than a nebulous force referred to as "the people." This sudden shift produced inevitable upheaval. In addition, the Mexicans could not seem to settle upon one form of republican government. At the time of independence, they preferred extreme decentralization. Then,

in the mid-1830s, they changed their minds and created a tightly cen-
tralized federal government.

Provinces on the outskirts of the Mexican nation reacted
most violently to the idea of direct control from Mexico City. Texas,
with a majority of settlers from the United States, declared its independence rather than submit. And California did as well. Yet California and Texas had divergent outcomes to their declarations of independence. Mexico sent an army to subdue the Texans. It destroyed an
Anglo-American force at the Alamo before losing the major battle of
that war at San Jacinto. Mexico then retreated, claiming still to pos-
sess Texas despite the reality of Texan independence. California's
scenario was more complicated.

In California, local Mexicans (Californios) themselves led
the secessionist movement. Yet not all Californios were in favor of
independence. Those living in northern California tended to favor
separation from Mexico. They were led by Juan Bautista Alvarado
and José Castro, who both expelled the Mexican governor and opposed Mexican centralization. Alvarado then became the new Californio governor, but Californios in southern California were dis-
pleased with this turn of events. The distance between the capital at
Monterey and Los Angeles, the principal city in the south, bred dis-
trust. Angelenos suspected that the northern Californios in an independent Californio republic would ignore southern California and
hoard the income from the customs house in Monterey for their own
benefit. In addition, Angelenos held out hope that their opposition
might win a transfer of the capital from Monterey to Los Angeles as a
reward for remaining loyal to Mexico.

Mexico's action at this juncture was to minimize the revolt in
California. Cleverly, it recognized the secessionist Alvarado as the
legal Mexican governor and pretended that nothing had happened.
For all intents and purposes, Alvarado's California was independent,
but Mexico acted as if it was still part of the Mexican nation. At that
moment, Mexico's full attention and energies were focused on Texas.
The fact that Texas's seceders were primarily Anglo-American made
Mexican toleration of them impossible. Anglo-American expansionism had long been feared, and in Texas it was clearly apparent. In
contrast to its reaction to the Texan declaration, Mexico treated California with utmost caution.

Alvarado went along with the legal fiction that California
remained part of Mexico, a course of action which enabled him to

minimize the unfortunate split between northern and southern Californios. He was the "Mexican" governor of a California that acted as if it was independent. With the passage of years, passions cooled; and in 1842 Mexico sent a new governor ostensibly to revive Mexican authority in the distant province. Mañuel Micheltorena, the new governor, arrived with 300 tough soldiers who were mostly former convicts. These quickly alienated the Californio population by their disorderly behavior. These "cholos," as they were derisively called by the Californios, helped reawaken Californio dreams of complete independence.

Ironically, the new Mexican governor sought the favor of Americans present in the area to help counterbalance local Californio opposition. Micheltorena endured the humiliation of Commodore Jones temporarily seizing his capital and then subsequently gave land grants to Anglo-Americans such as John Bidwell to win their supposed loyalty against his Californio rivals. As Micheltorena attempted to buy American support with land grants, northern and southern Californios came together against a common enemy—Governor Micheltorena and his hated band of convict-soldiers.

Alvarado and Castro met with Californio leaders in Los Angeles and from there both groups announced themselves against Micheltorena, who marched his forces south to encounter his enemies. Americans in southern California sensed that Micheltorena would lose the forthcoming military encounter and backed Alvarado's new rebellion. On February 20, 1845, the Battle of Cahuenga Pass began on the northern outskirts of Los Angeles. Reluctant to fight against each other, Americans and other foreigners on both sides decided to withdraw from the conflict and let Micheltorena and his enemies fight it out on their own. Thereupon, after several days of stand-off, the Mexican governor felt that he had no choice but to capitulate, such was his reliance upon his foreign mercenaries. Micheltorena and his "cholo" army left California for good. As a result of the Battle of Cahuenga Pass, well over a year before the beginning of the United States' war with Mexico, California again was an independent province under Californio leadership.

For their part, the Californios decided to divide the governmental duties among themselves. Pío Pico of Los Angeles became governor, and he moved the capital to Los Angeles on his own authority. José Castro, representing the northern Californios, acquired managerial control over the customs house at Monterey, the source of

all incoming tax revenues paid by the Yankee ship captains among
others. The southern Californios had only an authority based upon
exalted titles, but the northern Californios had the real power of control over the province's treasury.

Alvarado's uncle, Mariano Guadalupe Vallejo, observed
these events from his rancho on the northern reaches of San Francisco
Bay. He was disgusted by all of the factionalism and intrigue that
promised to continue either under Mexican or Californio rule. He
concluded that neither Pico, Castro, Alvarado, nor any future Mexican governor was California's best hope. Instead, he prayed for the
United States (then seen by some as the inevitable eventual owner of
the province) as California's best chance for stable government. Ironically, when an American move to seize the province finally occurred,
the first strike was against Vallejo's own rancho. Then, its pro-
American owner would be taken captive by the Americans; and from
the vantage point of a prisoner Vallejo would see his wish come true.

The month following the Battle of Cahuenga Pass between
Mexican authority and the Californios, the United States annexed the
Republic of Texas, which had successfully maintained an independent existence for almost a decade. Mexico had not recognized the
Republic of Texas any more than it had recognized the de facto independence of California. Accordingly, Mexico interpreted the American action as an act of war and promptly broke diplomatic relations.
The American president, James K. Polk, bided his time, expecting
that the break in diplomatic relations would eventually result in a war
with Mexico, in which he could seize the province of California. But
he brooded about the possibility of a British-Mexican alliance that
might foil his plans. Accordingly, Polk ordered John Charles Frémont, an officer in the U.S. Army's Topographical Corps, to lead a
force of 60 well armed men to California to provide at least a small
American professional fighting force on the scene to obstruct the
British from interfering with his perception of Anglo-American destiny.

Frémont's arrival at Monterey early in 1846 was viewed with
great suspicion by José Castro, who not only controlled the customs
house but also doubled as California's military leader. Castro ordered
Frémont away from the coast, but the brash American resisted, only
to retire when a superior Californio force was raised against him.
From Monterey, the humiliated Frémont retreated into the interior,
where at Sutter's Fort he ignited the growing Anglo-American pio-

neer population gathered there with tales of how he had not been allowed to stay on the coast to keep an eye on the British. From there, Frémont continued northward toward Oregon, reasoning that he could monitor British intentions in that quarter, where a possible war between England and the United States was brewing over the two nations' joint claim to the Oregon Country.

But Frémont halted his northern advance when a secret American agent caught up to him, informing him of the growing certainty of war between Mexico and the United States. Returning to Sacramento, Frémont's very presence encouraged revolution. The time was the early summer of 1846. Hot-headed American farmers there decided to take events into their own hands and proclaimed the existence of a "California Republic" under Anglo-American control. In fact, war between Mexico and United States had already begun along the Rio Grande, but neither the American rebels in California nor Frémont knew of this for sure. Far from his superiors and feeling the necessity to take sides as the rebels made their plans, Frémont resigned his commission in the U.S. Army and joined the so-called "Bear Flag Revolt," named after the banner that the rebels designed for their cause. The seizure of Vallejo and his rancho was one of their first acts. Within a month, news arrived of the greater conflict between the United States and Mexico; and the Bear Flag Revolt was absorbed into the official American military effort intent on seizing the province. In this manner, amidst violence, bloodshed and anger, the Mexican period of California history came to a close.

In coming years, Californio influence would first weaken and then be effectively smothered by an Anglo-American avalanche of newcomers. Most Anglo-Americans showed the Californios little respect. But a similar process had transpired during the Mexican period, this one involving the rapid dissolution of California's Indians at the hands of the Californios themselves who had little respect for these Indians, although many of the former carried more than traces of Native American ancestry in their familial origins rooted in Mexico. Their use of the term "cholo" to refer to Micheltorena's soldiers indicated a racism present even in Mexican culture. While the Spanish way had been to allow all racial groups the opportunity of becoming "gente de razon," none appeared to reach the status of truly reasonable people as completely as those of European racial origin. "Cholo" is a term that blends both behavioral and racial characteristics in its meaning. It means both "cowardly" and "half-breed." It is usually reserved for "half-civilized" Indians. Whereas Anglo-American racism would be even more stark, racial contempt for those not fully Spanish was also present in nineteenth-century Mexico and Mexican California.

Freed from the missions, California's Indians faced this racism without the paternalistic protectiveness that had characterized many of the deposed mission fathers. Weakened and disoriented by the mission experience, many freed Indians turned readily to alcohol. Any lands that they acquired in the secularization process were quickly lost. In 1844, the city government of Los Angeles passed an ordinance requiring all residents to have employment. The measure was aimed at the city's Indians. Those not finding work were arrested and put to work on city projects or leased out to private parties. The virtual slavery of the mission system had ended, but a new form of peonage had arisen in its place. Meanwhile, alcoholism and disease continued to take their toll. In 1852, four years after the conclusion of the American conquest, there were 3,693 Indians living in Los Angeles. By 1860, there were only 2,014; and by 1870, a meager 219. After California's inclusion in the United States, the decline of the Californios themselves was less precipitous but no less certain.

Suggestions for Further Reading

1. David J. Weber, "Failure of a Frontier Institution: The Secular Church in the Borderlands Under Independent Mexico, 1821-1846," *Western Historical Quarterly*, 12 (April 1981), 125-44.

2. James A. Sandos, "Levantamiento! The Chumash Uprising Reconsidered," *Southern California Quarterly*, 67 (Summer 1985), 109-34.

3. George Harwood Phillips, "Indians in Los Angeles, 1781-1875: Economic Integration, Social Disintegration," *Pacific Historical Review*, 49 (August 1980), 427-52.

4. John A. Hawgood, "The Pattern of Yankee Infiltration in Mexican Alta California, 1821-1846," *Pacific Historical Review*, 27 (February 1958), 27-38.

5. Robert Glass Cleland, *This Reckless Breed of Men: The Trappers and Fur Traders of the Southwest* (1952).

6. Gene A. Smith, "Thomas ap Catesby Jones and the First Implementation of the Monroe Doctrine," *Southern California Quarterly.* 76 (Spring 1994), 139-52.

7. Charles B. Churchill, "Thomas Jefferson Farnham: An Exponent of American Empire in Mexican California," *Pacific Historical Review*, 60 (November 1991), 517-37.

8. Irving Stone, *Men to Match My Mountains: The Opening of the Far West, 1840-1900* (1956).

9. Alan Rosenus, *General M.G. Vallejo and the Advent of the Americans: A Biography* (1995).

10. Russell M. Posner, "A British Consular Agent in California: The Reports of James A. Forbes, 1843-1846," *Southern California Quarterly*, 53 (June 1971), 101-12.

11. Douglas Monroy, *Thrown Among Strangers: The Making of Mexican Culture in Frontier California* (1991).

12. David J. Weber, *The Mexican Frontier, 1821-1846; The American Southwest Under Mexico* (1982).

13. Tony Stanley Cook, "Historical Mythmaking: Richard Henry Dana and American Immigration to California, 1840-1850," *Southern California Quarterly*, 68 (Summer 1986), 97-118.

14. Howard R. Lamar, with an Introduction by Kenneth N. Owens, "John Augustus Sutter, Wilderness Entrepreneur." *California History*, 73 (Summer 1994), 98-113.

15. James A. Sandos, "Between Crucifix and Lance: Indian-White Relations in California, 1765-1848," *California History*, 76 (Summer and Fall 1997), 196-229.

16. Doyce B. Nunis, Jr., "Alta California's Trojan Horse: Foreign Immigration," *California History*, 76 (Summer and Fall 1997), 299-330.

V
CALIFORNIA'S "MANIFEST DESTINY"

In the 1840s, President James K. Polk acquired California for the United States. Many Americans at the time celebrated this outcome as both inevitable and willed by God. Even today, many believe that it was at least inevitable, whether or not Divine Providence was involved. There are few if any modern historians who idealize Polk's accomplishment, but even those who view his imperialistic policy as wrongheaded overwhelmingly regard the American acquisition of California as virtually inevitable. Persisting into modern times, the apparent universality of this assumption is fascinating.

Americans of the time spoke of their nation's "Manifest Destiny," by which they meant that it was inevitable that some day the American Union would spread from sea to sea and possibly from pole to pole. It is common knowledge that the 1840s was the decade when American expansionism reached its apex. And the conquest of California occurred within that ideological context. Although most modern Americans sneer at the concept of "Manifest Destiny" as both arrogant and racist, they apparently still believe in principal aspects of it; for if one holds that California inevitably became part of the United States, then at least a partial faith in "Manifest Destiny" is revealed.

The origins of thinking in terms of "manifest destiny" are ancient. Hebrew scriptures assumed divine historical providence (i.e., manifest destiny). Yet the term "Manifest Destiny," as it was understood in the 1840s, had a more modern, social-scientific twist. In the late eighteenth and early nineteenth centuries, as people increasingly witnessed the wonders wrought by new technological advances, the concept of inevitable material progress became the intellectual rage throughout western civilization. German philosophers translated the ancient Hebraic assumption of divine omnipotence into the more modern natural laws of human history. Immanuel Kant (1724-1804), George Wilhelm Friedrich Hegel (1770-1831) and Karl Marx (1818-1883) are most famous for their arguments concerning the inevitable progressive march of history toward human perfection in socio-economic relationships. Nineteenth-century thinkers were enthralled by the idea of humanity reaching to higher and higher levels of material prosperity. Yet within this seemingly optimistic philosophy was at least one negative thought. These same thinkers portrayed human beings as the playthings of historical forces beyond their own control.

Despite the grand philosophical assumptions behind the concept of Manifest Destiny, it was not inevitable that the United States acquire California. Had it not been for a few thousand votes in the presidential election of 1844, the westward expansion of the nation would have been stalled for at least four years, if not longer. And once delayed, the concept of Manifest Destiny might have undergone interesting mutations, resulting in perhaps an inevitable late-nineteenth-century dominance of Anglo-Americans from coast to coast, but not necessarily under the stars and stripes. It takes just a little historical imagination to see the emergence of several Anglo-American nations in place of the one that eventually filled out much of the North American continent. This kind of counterfactual speculation is disreputable in some academic circles, but it is absolutely essential if one is to be disabused of the unconscious and unwarranted assumption that California became part of the United States as a result of some inevitable historical process.

In 1844, the presidential contestants in the United States were the Whig Henry Clay and the Democrat James K. Polk. The latter had served as Speaker of the House but was relatively unknown when compared to Clay. Polk ran on a platform of Manifest Destiny and promised that if he became president, the United States would annex both the Republic of Texas and the Oregon Country. He made no public promises regarding California; but if both Texas and Oregon were acquired, California could not be far behind. By contrast, Clay was anti-expansion, believing that rapid territorial growth only served to heat up the slavery issue, which was already tearing the country apart. The Louisiana Purchase of 1803 had already demonstrated that territorial expansion led to angry arguments over whether the acquired area should be open or closed to slavery. In addition to encouraging domestic turmoil over slavery, Polk's proposal of adding both Texas and Oregon within four years threatened the United States with a two-front war, involving both Mexico and Great Britain. Certainly, Mexico would go to war rather than peacefully submit to a *norteamericano* annexation of Texas; and Great Britain would not surrender her joint claim to the Oregon Country without a fight.

In one of the closest elections in American history, Polk defeated Clay. In New York state, the switch of 5,080 votes from a third party (devoted to the single issue of the abolition of slavery) to Clay

would have made the latter president between 1845 and 1849. As
most of the 15,812 New York adherents to this third party were normally Whigs, their votes literally denied the presidency to Henry
Clay. If Manifest Destiny did indeed exist, it was an historical inevitability that rested on a little more than 5,000 votes, out of over two
and a half million cast.

Polk's election and the subsequent annexation of Texas im-

Texas and Oregon
Presidential Campaign of 1844

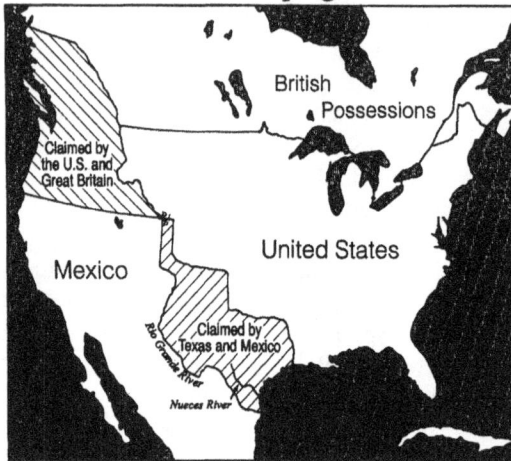

mediately produced a situation threatening war between Mexico and
the United States. Tensions between the United States and England
also mounted. Early in his presidency, Polk demanded that the United
States get all of the Oregon Country up to 54 degrees, 40 minutes
latitude, the southern boundary of Russian Alaska. This brazen proposal of "54-40 or fight" unrealistically suggested that powerful England get nothing for her joint claim. Polk was clearly pushing the
United States toward a feared two-front war. Simultaneously, Polk
ordered the U.S. Army to take up positions on the Rio Grande, an act
which goaded the Mexican nation to respond with force. By Mexican
law, the southern boundary of the department of Texas was the Nue-
ces River, well to the north of the Rio Grande. From the Mexican
view, the U.S. Army had invaded Mexico proper, beyond the traditional boundaries of Texas, leaving no choice but to fight.

Meanwhile, other developments created possibilities regarding the future control of the West. The Church of Jesus Christ of Latter Day Saints, or Mormons, resolved to move en masse to California. In June of 1844, the Mormon leader Joseph Smith had been killed by an Illinois mob. This was the last of a long string of incidents that convinced many Mormons that they were not welcome in the United States. Brigham Young, their new leader, resolved to lead an exodus out the United States into the Mexican territory called California. At that time, "California" referred to that which is today not only California, but also Nevada and Utah. Young was silent concerning his exact destination, and this ambiguity created anxiety among both the Californios and Anglo-American settlers in California. Polk became nervous as well. Well before the beginning of the Mexican War, rumors of this mass Mormon migration were circulating in the eastern press. Polk's own party newspaper joined in the warnings. If the Mormon faithful answered Young's call in the numbers expected, the Latter Day Saints could quickly match and surpass the existing numbers of both Californios and non-Mormon Anglo-Americans in California. Under such conditions, a separate Mormon nation in California seemed likely.

In the war that began along the Rio Grande in May of 1846, California was conquered by the U.S. Army as a prize of war well before Brigham Young could get his exodus underway. However, without all of these expansionist events resulting from the close presidential election of 1844, one can well imagine Young erecting an independent theocracy on the western slope of the Rocky Mountains. This outcome would not have been the Manifest Destiny of James K. Polk. With the Mormons established in "California," a future expansionistic United States would have had to deal with a more formidable force than they faced in Mexican California in 1846. Possibly, only Polk's paper-thin victory over Clay prevented this development.

Another occurrence was not inevitable—that being the peaceful resolution of the dispute with Great Britain over Oregon, which enabled the United States to fight Mexico without any English involvement. One can only imagine the outcome of a war with Great Britain in alliance with Mexico. In his negotiations with Great Britain over Oregon, Polk had shown himself to be as inflexible as he was with Mexico over Texas. Polk's tough stance over Oregon was popular with anti-slavery expansionists. But given the certainty of war with Mexico, Polk eventually moderated his Oregon position and compromised by dividing the Oregon Country at the 49th parallel, the northern boundary of the present-day state of Washington. Free soilers felt betrayed.

Polk's options had not been ideal. Either he could risk the disaster of a two-front war, or he could guarantee internal sectional strife by his presumed preference to expand slavery at the expense of free soil. He chose the latter path which immediately avoided a two-front war and led to a relatively quick victory in the Mexican War. But it also led toward eventual civil war within his own country.

Polk had run for the presidency with the promise that he would acquire all of the territory claimed by Texas as well as the disputed Oregon Country. "All of Texas" had appealed to slavery's expansionists. "All of Oregon" had appealed to those who wanted an equivalent amount of free soil to neutralize the political impact of a new slave state in Texas. Polk went to war over Texas, but he compromised his demand concerning Oregon. This action seriously damaged Northern faith in southern slave-holder politicians. Polk himself was a Tennessee slave-holder, and after the Oregon compromise the war was billed in the North as a war to expand slavery. It was clear that Polk intended to take California and that slavery might expand westward as a result. In opposition to this possibility, New England's Henry David Thoreau developed his philosophy of civil disobedience, which would later influence both Mahatma Gandhi and Martin Luther King, Jr.

Meanwhile, California's supposed manifest destiny was taking shape in the Far West. As was shown in the last chapter, Polk's prewar anxieties early in his presidency had led him to send John Charles Frémont's small force to California. Arriving in California early in 1846, Frémont reflected his president's concern regarding British intentions in California. Frémont's principal objective was to keep an eye on possible British intrigues in California's capital. Accordingly, he resisted the Californio demand that he move his force away from Monterey and the coast. Eventually, Frémont reluctantly moved into the interior valleys, after being forced to leave the coastal area by a Californio militia. Frustrated in his principal objective, Frémont raged to Anglo-American settlers in the interior. His emotion fueled the passions of hot-heads. The result was the Bear Flag Revolt.

The flag of the rebels subsequently became the official state flag and to this day flies over all state buildings. African Americans have long been offended by representations of the defeated Confederate flag on many Southern state flags, claiming that these are symbols of slavery and directly or indirectly honor those who fought to protect and sustain that hated institution. By contrast, modern Latino Californians have yet to make a similar issue over the continuing presence of the Bear flag in their state. The Bear flag is one of the few enduring historical symbols that one sees every day in a rapidly changing California.

The Bear Flaggers never got far beyond Mariano Guadalupe Vallejo's rancho in the north bay region. From a military standpoint, they were insignificant and never involved more than a few hundred men. As soon as the U.S. Navy arrived at Monterey, bringing news of the Mexican War, these rebels were incorporated into the American military effort. With the authority of the United States backing them, Frémont and his former Bear Flaggers moved southward and raised the American flag in every major locale without incident. But the arrogant attitude of the small Anglo-American garrison left to hold Los Angeles produced a delayed reaction among the Californio population there. On September 23, 1846, the citizenry rose in rebellion and put the limited American forces there under siege. Other southern California towns likewise rose upon this example; and soon, that which had appeared so easily won, was lost. Southern California was unwilling to accept Manifest Destiny without a fight.

Polk's original plan for the conquest of California called for a U.S. army contingent under General Stephen Watts Kearny to move overland from Ft. Leavenworth, Kansas, through Santa Fe, New Mexico, and into southern California. Kearny had been dispatched in June; but upon hearing about the quick success in subduing California by the forces on hand, he had elected to enter California with only 200 men. On December 5, at San Pascual, near present-day Escondido, Kearny's men met about 150 Californios under the command of Andrés Pico, the brother of Governor Pío Pico. Kearny got the worst of the conflict, for the Californio militia constituted a skilled calvary force, enjoying a superior mobility over their enemy.

Taking up defensive positions, Kearny sent out a plea for help which was answered by several hundred marines and sailors who arrived from Monterey by sea and rushed to rescue the beleaguered U.S. Army after a week of siege. Faced with these new odds, the Californios retreated; and the Battle of San Pascual was over. Everywhere but Los Angeles, Californio resistance was broken by superior

American numbers. Californio independence also ended there on January 10, 1847, after which the fighting was virtually over in California. Just outside Los Angeles Andrés Pico finally surrendered his force to Frémont on January 13.

Two weeks later, the so-called Mormon Battalion arrived in San Diego after a trek following Kearny's route overland. This U.S. Army contingent of Mormon volunteers made up part of Kearny's overall command. Cleverly, Polk had chosen to co-opt a potential enemy in assisting the American conquest of California. The Mormon recruits sent their pay checks to Brigham Young, thus helping to finance the Mormon exodus west. In this way, Polk linked Mormon interests to those of the United States. Had Clay been elected president in 1844, all would have been different. As it was, by the time that Brigham Young established a Mormon presence near the Great Salt Lake in Utah, the area was part of the United States. On February 2, 1848, the United States and Mexico signed the Treaty of Guadalupe Hidalgo; and the Mexican War was over. Only in hindsight can it appear that all of this was California's "Manifest Destiny."

Despite the controversial nature of this war, the American public hungrily identified heroes to celebrate this history. General Zachary Taylor, a victor of battles in Mexico, was chosen to replace Henry Clay as the Whig standard bearer in 1848. In California, John C. Frémont also took on heroic stature in the eyes of many. For his own part, Frémont wanted to leave no question in the public mind that he had been the indispensable man in California.

Once absorbed into the American war effort, Frémont was required to abandon his reckless freebooter activities as a Bear Flagger. At first, he followed orders, while being allowed much latitude by his commanding officer, Commodore Robert Stockton, who commanded the U.S. Navy in California. Before Kearny's arrival overland, Frémont was the top Army man in the province. But with Kearny on the scene, this ended. Impetuously, Frémont refused to defer to Kearny and became openly insubordinate. Finally, Kearny arrested the upstart and took him east to face a court martial, which dismissed him from the army. President Polk necessarily backed the verdict.

Yet Frémont was not broken by this turn of events. All of the publicity surrounding the trial built Frémont's reputation as the crucial man in California's conquest. After California was given statehood, Frémont parlayed his fame into becoming one of California's first U.S. Senators. In the Senate, he stood out as a vociferous opponent of slavery's expansion. Instantly, he had cast himself into an ideal role—a hero from a war supposedly begun to expand slavery, who nonetheless personally was opposed to slavery. His constant self-promotion made him a hot political property in the volatile decade of the 1850s.

Immanuel Kant had written that man was created by Nature (Divine Providence) to be in perpetual conflict for the advancement of humanity. He had prophesied that the most energetic of available contestants would survive and that slackers would fail. Inevitable progress would thereby result. He claimed that this rule of existence defined both individual biographies and the histories of nations. Frémont intended himself to be the primary beneficiary of Manifest Destiny. In his own mind, California had been conquered because of his energy; and as his country was a nation of destiny, he was a man of destiny. California's acquisition propelled him onto a national stage; and in 1856, he became the new Republican Party's first candidate for the Presidency. Unsuccessful in that campaign, he later served as a general in the Union Army during the Civil War. Yet he never again achieved a notoriety equal to that which he had enjoyed when cast in the role as California's conqueror. The details of his individual history did not ultimately transpire to produce a seemingly inevitable success as perfectly as did those events leading to the American acquisition of California.

Suggestions for Further Reading

1. Anders Stephenson, *Manifest Destiny: American Expansionism and the Empire of Right* (1995).

2. Bernard DeVoto, *The Year of Decision, 1846* (1942).

3. Ward M. McAfee and J. Cordell Robinson, eds. and trans., *Origins of the Mexican War, A Documentary Source Book*, 2 vols. (1982).

4. Andrew Rolle, "Exploring an Explorer: Psychohistory and John Charles Frémont," *Pacific Historical Review*, 51 (May 1982), 135-64.

5. John A. Hawgood, "John C. Frémont and the Bear Flag Revolution," *Southern California Quarterly*, 49 (June 1962), 67-96.

6. Jack K. Baur, *The Mexican War, 1846-1848* (1993).

7. Neal Harlow, *California Conquered: War and Peace on the Pacific, 1846-1850* (1982).

8. Susan Easton Black, "The Mormon Battalion: Conflict Between Religious and Military Authority," *Southern California Quarterly*, 74 (Winter 1992), 313-28.

9 Albert L. Hurtado, "Controlling California's Indian Labor Force: Federal Administration of California Indian Affairs During the Mexican War," *Southern California Quarterly*, 61 (Fall 1979), 217-38.

10. Richard Griswold del Castillo, *The Treaty of Guadalupe Hidalgo* (1990).

11. Lisbeth Haas, "War in California, 1846-1848," *California History* (Summer and Fall 1997), 331-60.

VI

CALIFORNIA'S INSTABILITY AND THE COMING OF THE CIVIL WAR

Historians have long debated what caused the American Civil War, which lasted from 1861 to 1865. Slavery and rapid industrialization are some of the more familiar reasons given. Instability emanating from California was yet another cause. Certainly, California was not as important as slavery or rapid industrialization in the causation of the Civil War. Nevertheless, California was intimately involved in the principal events that led to the most terrible conflict in American history. The Compromise of 1850, the Kansas-Nebraska Act of 1854, the birth of the Republican Party, and the Dred Scott decision—all are familiar to Civil War historians. All involved California, directly or indirectly.

In the last chapter, we saw how Henry Clay had feared that rapid western expansion would heat up the slavery issue and make internal trouble for the young United States. His fears were warranted. Even before the American conquest was finalized in the Treaty of Guadalupe Hidalgo, Polk's expansionist policies had unleashed a new torrent of sectionalism which greatly worried the nation's leaders.

In 1848, President-elect Zachary Taylor planned to leave California and New Mexico undeveloped, in hopes that this might cool sectional conflict over the Mexican Cession's future course. Once a bill was presented in Congress proposing to organize these conquered territories officially into territorial governments and to establish American institutions in them by law, the slavery issue was certain to boil. Taylor intended to forestall any such event. The new president reasoned that both California and New Mexico were sleepy Mexican backwaters with miniscule populations and were unworthy of even territorial government. Military administration of the Mexican or Californio laws in existence at the time of conquest promised that both California and New Mexico could remain reasonably static. In this manner, Taylor hoped to defuse the slavery issue, at least temporarily.

Taylor's plan never had an opportunity to play itself out. News of a discovery of gold near Sutter's Fort, arriving late in 1848, undermined all of his assumptions. The American soldiers, who under

Taylor's plan were to administer Mexican and Californio law, deserted to the gold fields. Anarchy reigned as young men from around the world set out for San Francisco on their own expeditions to acquire California's gold. Almost overnight, California lost the genteel pace of change that had characterized both the Spanish and Mexican periods. From this moment on, California history became extremely dynamic.

Ad-hoc justice ruled the gold fields. The racism of Anglo-American and European miners had no effective check. White miners drove out rival gold seekers from Mexico and China. Indians were brushed aside, abused and killed. Lawyers, or anyone else who might complain against mob rule, were driven from the fields. Clearly, there was a need for government. Taylor was forced to acknowledge that some proposal for bringing regular law to California had to be made, thereby risking an angry intersectional debate over whether California should be slave or free. Quickly, the new president dispatched an emissary to try to direct events in volatile California.

Even before the arrival of Taylor's representative, elections were held for a state constitutional convention, which met at Monterey in 1849. Both Anglo-Americans and Californios were represented. They drew boundaries for California, choosing to define an eastern boundary close to the far side of the Sierra Nevadas. This was done to restrict the unavoidable conflict over the slavery issue. Also, the convention decided that California would be a free state and that black people would be banned from entering the new El Dorado. At that time, white racism and anti-slavery often marched hand in hand. In opposing slavery, some white people maliciously wanted to recreate a United States with no economic role for African Americans. This attitude was dominant in the Monterey convention. The new California constitution was sent to Congress for approval.

Taylor hoped that by skipping the normal intermediary stage of territorial government, California might not generate a sectional crisis. Historical precedent suggested that Congress could only determine the status of slavery in organized territories. In the past, only Northerners had ever questioned a new state's right of self-determination on this issue. In 1819, Northern Congressmen's resistance to Missouri's application to become a slave state had produced a national crisis that had resulted in the Missouri Compromise of 1820. That compromise had admitted Missouri as a slave state and prohibited slavery in the old Louisiana Purchase area north of 36 degrees,

30 minutes, parallel. Given that in the Missouri crisis Southerners had roundly criticized Northern interference with Missouri's right to determine its own domestic institutions, Taylor hoped that Southerners would stay consistent now that California was applying for statehood

or
lic
m
e>
be
ar
hi
hi
th
H
se
ha
sl

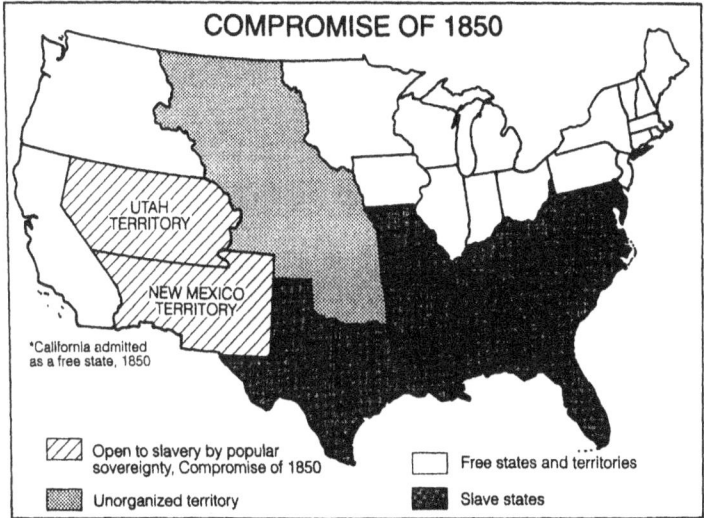

er
id
pl

COMPROMISE OF 1850

UTAH TERRITORY

NEW MEXICO TERRITORY

*California admitted as a free state, 1850

Open to slavery by popular sovereignty, Compromise of 1850

Unorganized territory

Free states and territories

Slave states

fused to follow his presidential leadership. As a general, he had grown accustomed to subordinates following orders. The nation was headed for a political crisis generated by California's Gold Rush, and the existing national leadership seemed incapable of heading off disaster. Then, suddenly, Taylor died. A young, energetic Senator Stephen A. Douglas of Illinois succeeded in passing the various elements making up Clay's so-called Compromise of 1850. The new president, Millard Fillmore, signed the measures; and the crisis appeared to be over. But the renewed sectional peace was only a facade.

Throughout the remainder of the decade, Northerners ignored the new Fugitive Slave Act, with some Northern states even officially nullifying the law. Indeed, Harriet Beecher Stowe wrote *Uncle Tom's Cabin*, a best-selling novel encouraging this Northern nullification. Outraged and alienated, Southerners complained that the North had added California to its sectional domain, but the South received nothing meaningful in exchange. Given the North's effective reneging on the supposed deal of 1850, Southerners argued that they deserved at least half of California. Later in the decade, their attitude encouraged an effort to split the new state in two.

That which transpired in 1849-1850 alone could make a case that California helped cause the Civil War that finally erupted in 1861. But there was more than just this. Talk of building a transcontinental railroad to connect California with trunk lines in the East also encouraged sectional conflict. Powerful commercial interests demanded progress. Californians themselves exacerbated matters by threatening secession unless federal action in facilitating a transcontinental line occurred quickly. California's population at that time was young. Men in their twenties were the norm. Few women had come west in the Gold Rush, and California's young men were lonely, deeply lonely. From their perspective, they were lost at the end of the earth. One popular song among the miners stated: "I wish I was but back again; how altered I would be! I'd appreciate the pretty girls, whom I could always see. But 'tween me and those lovely girls the billowy oceans roar." Home seemed so far away. They believed that young women would come west in sufficient numbers only when a transcontinental railroad was completed. These virile Californians

WHAT WE WANT IN CALIFORNIA.

FROM NEW-YORK DIRECT

FAMILY AND FIRE-SIDE

LITH. & PUB. BY BRITTON & REY   SAN FRANCISCO

knew their power. They had seen soldiers desert their posts to become
miners. They believed that the United States had no ability to stop
them in carrying out their threat of secession, should they choose to
exercise it. Any army sent against them, commented one young Californian, "would disappear like a lump of salt in a rain storm."

California's Population by Gender (Thousands)			
Year	Male	Female	Female % of Total
1850	86	7	7.5
1860	273	107	28.2
1870	349	211	37.7
1880	518	347	40.1
1890	703	511	42.1
1900	821	665	44.8
1910	1,323	1,055	44.4
1920	1,814	1,613	47.1
1930	2,943	2,735	48.2
1940	3,516	3,392	49.1
1950	5,296	5,291	49.98

Women were a minority in California during the American period up until the
1950s, when they became the majority in the state. (Data from U.S. Department
of Commerce, *Historical Statistics of the United States, Colonial Times to
1970*. 2 vols. Vol. 1., p. 25).

In the early 1850s, Mississippi's Jefferson Davis (later to become the president of the Confederacy during the Civil War) was the
United States Secretary of War and in this capacity supervised the
Army Corps of Engineers. His surveyors reported to him that the best
of all possible railroad routes to California would traverse the extreme South and terminate in San Diego. This report was grounded in
solid geographic evidence, although it was politically suspect because
of Davis' own bias toward the South. The route bypassed the obsta-
cles of the Sierra Nevada and Rocky Mountain chains. Its major flaw
was that part of it dipped into Mexican territory. Accordingly, Davis
arranged for the administration of Franklin Pierce to negotiate the
purchase of the needed territory from Mexico, and the Gadsden Purchase was finalized in 1854. Initially, it appeared that the South had
an advantage in the discussion of feasible rail routes to California.

But Stephen Douglas of Illinois desperately wanted a more northerly route that would serve his state. His problem was that the old Louisiana Purchase Territory north of 36 degrees, 30 minutes, had never been organized into territories and opened to white settlement. Accordingly, a great swath of wilderness stood like a geographic wall barring any northern or even any central route to California. A transcontinental railroad could not be built through a wilderness where there would be no wayside customers to serve. Also, a new railroad would need protection from the Indians who then effectively dominated the wilderness region. Therefore, Douglas resolved to do whatever was necessary to organize the area into federal territories inviting settlers to move into the area.

Southern politicians had no interest in organizing the region, which was barred to slavery under the terms of the Missouri Compromise of 1820. Douglas, who cared little about the issue of slavery, saw no problem with this. To win Southern support, he proposed destroying the Missouri Compromise, creating two federal territories called Kansas and Nebraska, and allowing the people who moved to these territories to decide the slavery issue for themselves in their territorial legislatures. He called his solution to the political problem of resolving the slavery issue "popular sovereignty." His Kansas-Nebraska Act erased the historic demarcation line of 36 degrees, 30 minutes, and replaced Congressional control over slavery in the Louisiana Purchase area with local self-determination. Before slavery had been barred north of 36 degrees, 30 minutes by Congressional fiat. Douglas's bill made slavery's advance northward at least a possibility. His "popular sovereignty" solution convinced Southerners that they might pick up new territory for slavery. Hence, while the Kansas-Nebraska Act increased the possibility of a central railroad route to California, it did so at a terrible cost unforeseen by Douglas. He was actually surprised by his own section's moral outrage that followed what he regarded as a great legislative accomplishment.

Throughout the North, the act was seen as a capitulation to a "slave-power conspiracy" intent upon expanding slavery even into the North. Under the terms of the act, theoretically slavery could be extended all the way to the Canadian border if the people moving into the new territories so chose. In reaction to this possibility, a new political party came into existence which was pledged to preventing any westward expansion of slavery. Initially called the Anti-Kansas-Nebraska-Act Party, it quickly became known as the Republican

Party. In 1856, this new party backed its first presidential candidate, California's John Charles Frémont. Surprisingly, this first national campaign of the Republicans almost captured the presidency. Fear swept through Democratic Party ranks.

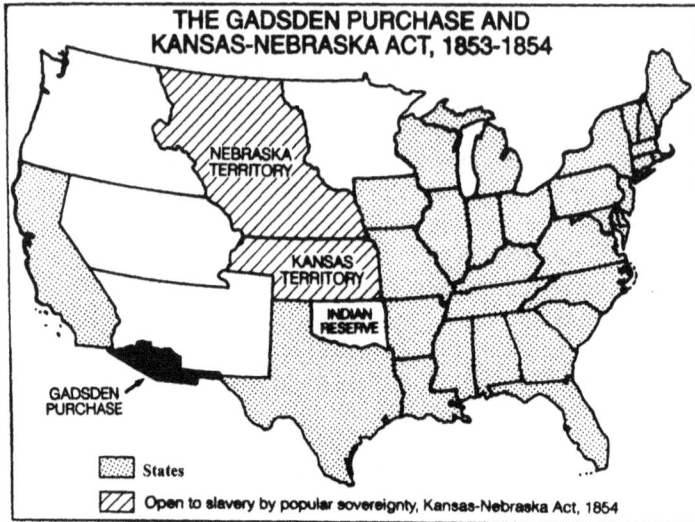

THE GADSDEN PURCHASE AND
KANSAS-NEBRASKA ACT, 1853-1854

NEBRASKA TERRITORY

KANSAS TERRITORY

INDIAN RESERVE

GADSDEN PURCHASE

States

Open to slavery by popular sovereignty, Kansas-Nebraska Act, 1854

Shortly afterward, the U.S. Supreme Court, then closely identified with the Democratic Party, handed down the infamous Dred Scott decision, informing the new Republican Party that it could not carry out its pledge to bar slavery from the western territories under the Constitution. By the Court's extreme and twisted interpretation of that fundamental document, Congress and even territorial governments had to allow slavery to come into all the western territories. California's insistence upon a transcontinental railroad had helped push the nation into a sectional confrontation over the possible extension of slavery into the western territories.

In addition to both the Compromise of 1850 and transcontinental railroad politics, California fed the growing sectionalism threatening to tear the nation apart. At the end of the decade, pro-Southern interests in California saw their opportunity to rectify what they regarded as the Northern betrayal in the Compromise of 1850. If California could be divided into two regions—a truncated California reduced to northern California alone and a new federal territory consisting of southern California—slavery could gain a foothold in southern California under the terms of the Dred Scott decision. Pro-Southern interests found an ally in southern California's Californio elite, which saw no future in the Anglo-dominated-state of California which was hostile to their large land holdings. High state taxes on land slowly were forcing Californio cattle barons to sell off their properties just to pay their taxes. In a separate southern California (which was then proposed to be called the "Territory of Colorado"), the Californio landed aristocracy believed that they might yet survive,

Andrés Pico, the hero of San Pascual, was one of the relatively few Californios still found in positions of influence a decade after the conquest. Courtesy, Huntington Library.

even with pro-slavery elements at their side. And under the terms of
the Dred Scott decision, slavery would have to be allowed to enter the
new "Territory of Colorado" (southern California).

Andrés Pico, the Californio hero of the Battle of San Pascual, led the movement to divide the state in 1859. By that time, the
state was controlled by the Democratic Party; and within the Democratic Party the most important element was pro-Southern. In California, this latter element was called the "Chiv" (Chivalry) Democracy.
Chiv Democrats were the power behind Pico's divide-the-state
movement. They succeeded in getting the state legislature to pass a
proposal splitting the state with San Luis Obispo and all counties
southward forming a new federal territory. Then, they presented the
measure only to southern California voters, whom they knew would
approve it. It was sent to Congress for final determination, but national Republican opposition buried it. This was the closest that the
state ever came to dividing.

In numerous other ways, California in the 1850s helped feed
the growing sectional conflict. A young Californian of Southern birth
named William Walker made repeated forays from San Francisco into
Central America attempting to conquer lands for slavery. For several
years in the mid-1850s, he succeeded in capturing control of Nicaragua with a small Anglo-American army, which he used to introduce
slavery there. Gold Rush California was filled with young adventur-
ers of this type. These California-based activities encouraged the belief of many Northerners that there was indeed a conspiracy afoot to
expand slavery. In time, the conspiratorial thesis went, these conquered lands would be annexed to the United States, as Texas had
been. Accordingly, this process was openly referred to as the "Texas
game." This belief drove more and more Northerners to back the Republican party. And this was not California's only additional contribution to national instability. In 1859, California's Chief Justice (David
S. Terry, a pro-slavery "Chiv" Democrat) killed one of California's
U.S. Senators (David Broderick, an anti-slavery Democrat) in an illegal duel. The incident, occurring on the eve of the Civil War, was
seen in the North as evidence of both the violent nature of pro-slavery
men and the need to stop their traditional control of American government.

The causation of any major event is necessarily complex and
involves many factors. But it cannot be denied that the acquisition of
California by the United States spelled trouble so far as maintaining

the nation's domestic tranquility was concerned. Throughout the decade, the new state was a continuous witness to anarchy and upheaval. The lack of "law and order" in this new state persuaded San Franciscans to administer vigilante justice, in which people suspected of crimes were arrested by citizens' committees and summarily executed. Everything in California's young masculine environment seemed to augur against peace and quiet. Southerners regularly held up California as an example of the failure of any society without a spirit of law and order which they claimed could only be maintained by the presence of slavery.

The Gold Rush, the brash nature of its young, male population, the fact that the South felt cheated by the Compromise of 1850 which had made California a state, all contributed to the sectional struggle that eventually ended in the bloodiest war in the nation's history. During the 1850s, California's history was closely intertwined with that of the troubled American nation which failed to resist the tidal pull toward civil war. California influenced this course of national events; and, in turn, the national drift toward civil war shaped California history.

Suggestions for Further Reading

1. John W. Caughey, *The California Gold Rush* (1975).

2. Albert L. Hurtado, *Indian Survival on the California Frontier* (1990).

3. Richard H. Peterson, "Anti-Mexican Nativism in California, 1848-1853," *Southern California Quarterly*, 62 (Winter 1980), 309-28.

4. Philip P. Choy, "Golden Mountain of Lead: The Chinese Experience in California," *California Historical Quarterly*, 50 (Sept. 1971), 267-76.

5. Rudolph M. Lapp, *Blacks in the California Gold Rush* (1977).

6. Jo Ann Levy, *They Saw the Elephant: Women in the California Gold Rush* (1992).

7. Robert M. Senkewicz, *Vigilantes in Gold Rush San Francisco* (1985).

8. Donald J. Pisani, "Squatter Law in California, 1850-1856," *Western Historical Quarterly*," 25 (Autumn 1994), 277-312.

9. Ronald C. Woolsey, "A Southern Dilemma: Slavery Expansion and the California Statehood Issues in 1850—A Reconsideration," *Southern California Quarterly*, 65 (Summer 1983), 123-44.

10. Arthur Quinn, *The Rivals: William Gwin, David Broderick, and the Birth of California* (1994).

11. Ward M. McAfee, "California History Textbooks and the Coming of the Civil War: The Need for a Broader Perspective of California History," *Southern California Quarterly*, 56 (Summer 1974), 159-70.

12. Ward M. McAfee, "California's House Divided," *Civil War History*, 33 (June 1987), 115-30.

13. Malcolm J. Rohrbough, *Days of Gold: The California Gold Rush and the American Nation* (c.1997).

VII
CALIFORNIA AND THE NEW UNION

Abraham Lincoln conducted the Civil War, which began shortly after his inauguration in 1861, on the premise that the Union was inviolate, or (in other words) that secession had not occurred. Yet it had happened in fact. Eleven Southern states proclaimed their separation from the United States and erected a new country entitled the Confederate States of America. As Lincoln began his first term, the nation was ruptured. In fact, the old Union of loosely connected states was dead. If the nation was to survive, it could only do so by methods alien to the way the old Union had been governed. Over the course of four bloody years, the Civil War forged a new nation; and California played an integral role in this drama.

One of Lincoln's first challenges upon taking office was to keep California in the Union. Throughout the 1850s, threats of secession had emanated from Californians themselves, frustrated with the federal government's dual inability to determine a transcontinental railroad route and provide modern transportation facilities for the Far West. With the creation of a self-proclaimed Southern Confederacy, its sympathizers along the Pacific coast argued that California (and possibly Oregon) should create a separate Pacific Republic, a move that would have aided the South by further fragmenting the damaged Union. Despite their anger with the old Union's inaction on railroad affairs, most Californians opposed secession. Republicans and most Democrats in the state rallied to Lincoln's cause to preserve the nation.

Secessionist sentiment existed only in pockets around the state. Southern California contained many pro-Southern advocates. But overall, Unionist feeling dominated. In 1861, Leland Stanford was elected California's first Republican governor. Lincoln and Stanford's Republican party pledged to get Congress to subsidize the construction of a first transcontinental railroad. Despite the South's alienation from the old Union over the slavery issue, Californians still had hope that Lincoln might deliver on railroad matters.

As the Southern states proclaimed their independence, their representatives and senators left the U.S. Congress. Here was Lincoln's opportunity. With only Northerners present in Congress, agreement upon a transcontinental railroad route was possible. In 1862, Congress passed the Pacific Railroad Act, providing the long awaited subsidy for a line to be built through the center of the country. The act provided that the Central Pacific Railroad (headed incidentally by California's Governor Stanford) would build from West to East, and the Union Pacific would build from East to West. Each company would get federal loans and a land grant of ten alternate sections of land for each mile of track laid. The act stipulated that the amount given in the loan would be more generous for mountainous terrain than flat land. Never before in American history had an internal improvement of this magnitude been undertaken by the federal government. Here was early evidence of the emergence of a new kind of Union.

Lincoln's promise to build a railroad across the continent was equivalent to President John Kennedy's pledge given a century later to land Americans on the moon. Both called forth a new consciousness. In the early 1860s, Lincoln's pledge imagined the creation of a new Union, bound together with rails of iron, indivisible. One major result of the Northern victory in the Civil War was to place nation over state—and national need over parochial interest, something new to the conception of the American Union. This understanding underwrote the idea that the Pacific Railroad Act was constitutional. A generation before, President Andrew Jackson had argued that any federal internal improvement of this scope was clearly inharmonious with a state-centered understanding of the Constitution. The Republicans favored a new idea of what was appropriate legislation within the Union, and the first transcontinental railroad symbolized the new primacy they gave to national sovereignty. A century later, the moon landings also called forth a new mentality. In our own time, the earth itself appears as a "new union," one planet indivisible.

Lincoln's challenge of creating a new Union required stretching the Constitution, as was done in the Pacific Railroad Act. Nevertheless, this first piece of legislation proved inadequate to the task at hand. The federal aid promised in the Pacific Railroad Act was not generous enough. And so Lincoln proclaimed that the Sierra Nevada mountains begin far to the west of where they actually are. He did this in order to grant larger loans immediately to the Central Pacific, as more money was forthcoming for track laid in mountainous terrain. Lincoln's proclamation was the act of a desperate president trying to make the project move forward. During the Civil War, iron and locomotives were at a premium due to the war effort. Enormous sums of money were needed to build a railroad. Much private capital investment was needed to make any meaningful progress on the line. Yet, despite the federal government's support, few capitalists put money into the Central Pacific. At the time, it was too great a risk. More immediate profits could be had by investing in other enterprises. Also, enemies of the railroad company charged that it was the "Dutch Flat Swindle," a supposed fraud intending only to build a short line into the Sierras and stop at a small mountain community named Dutch Flat, far short of its announced goal.

In 1864, in an effort to encourage needed private investment, Congress passed a second Pacific Railroad Act, which did two important things. It doubled the land grant to twenty alternate sections per mile constructed and stipulated that if the companies aided in the act went bankrupt, private investors (not the federal government itself) would have the first opportunity to retrieve their losses. In other words, the federal government's loans would only constitute a second (and inferior) mortgage. This finally persuaded San Francisco financiers to get behind the project.

In the early 1860s, San Francisco's capitalists had found that they could make easy profits by investing in manufacturing enterprises. Throughout the previous decade, little capital had been put into factories in San Francisco. Throughout the 1850s, San Franciscans had imported almost all that they needed from the East or abroad. The long sea voyage, necessitating waiting many months for goods, had resulted in wild fluctuations in prices. Supply and demand were difficult to keep in balance given California's extraordinarily long supply lines. Nonetheless, fortunes were made in commerce. Then the Civil War instantly created new opportunities for manufacturing, as opposed to trading in goods brought in from outside the state.

Great wars always disrupt shipping. Early in the nineteenth century, the Napoleonic Wars effectively had put normal trade between Europe and the United States on hold. One upshot of this had been the beginning of domestic manufacturing in the United States, to produce at home that which previously had been imported from abroad; and the American industrial revolution was born in the process. The Civil War had a similar effect upon San Francisco, which dramatically shifted toward manufacturing during the conflict. Locally manufactured goods were more expensive than Eastern or foreign items, but the former were available. Their production also produced jobs locally. As a result, San Francisco grew dramatically.

In 1860, its population had been only 57,000. By the end of the
decade, it was close to 160,000. In this boomtown environment, local
capitalists had been reluctant to invest in risky ventures such as the
Central Pacific Railroad. Easier returns could be gotten in
manufacturing.

While San Francisco was booming, southern California was
stagnating. Recurrent bouts with floods and drought decimated the
cattle industry there. Politics also served to sour the economy. More
than any other region in the state, southern California was cool toward preserving the Union. In 1859, the region had been for splitting
the state, a move which would have made southern California a federal territory open to slavery. Southern sympathizers predominated
among southern California's leading citizens. Ironically, Los Angeles'
Andrés Pico, who had fronted the split-the-state movement in 1859,
broke with his Southern friends in 1861 and became an ardent Lincoln supporter during the war. New possibilities for federal patronage
possibly accounted for his 180-degree political switch from Chiv
Democrat to Republican.

Early in the war, the Southern Confederacy made no secret
of its desire to conquer southern California for its own. The Battle of
Glorieta Pass, occurring near Santa Fe, New Mexico, in late March
1862, effectively ended that dream by beating back a westward Confederate advance. Nevertheless, southern California's Confederate
sympathizers refused to concede a Northern victory. The region's
Californio population also harbored a dark mood. The failure to split
California spelled their last hope to escape heavy state taxation of
their landed fiefdoms inherited from the Mexican period. Flooding,
followed by killing droughts, joined Mother Nature in a seeming
cosmic conspiracy to force Californio landholders into bankruptcy. In
contrast to San Francisco's boom of the 1860s, Los Angeles actually
registered a drop in property values in the decade.

Confederate forces failed to reach California by land, but
they continuously threatened by sea. San Francisco lay potentially
vulnerable to Confederate naval attack. One or two enemy vessels
getting through the decrepit harbor defenses promised terror for a
town most vulnerable to incendiary bombardment. In the 1850s, the
city had burned to the ground on numerous occasions. Close quarters
and wooden structures made San Francisco a tinderbox. Another
factor accounted for San Francisco's fear of Confederate battle
cruisers. California gold was shipped from the city by means of

Pacific Mail steamships. These vessels were a lure to Confederate privateers. California gold strengthened Federal finances vis-a-vis Confederate monetary management. The Confederacy had every reason to want to neutralize this advantage.

In October and November of 1863, a Russian fleet arrived in San Francisco and was welcomed as a godsend. This foreign flotilla came not to aid the Union defenses of the city, but to rest in a friendly neutral port. Fearing a general European war breaking out over its brutal handling of Polish insurrectionists, Russia moved its navy into friendly American waters during the height of the Civil War. Russia and the United States both feared foreign intervention in their affairs by the same powers—England and France. This gave Russia something in common with the United States, which San Franciscans celebrated during the winter of 1863-1864, when they regarded the Russian fleet as effectively protecting their city from Confederate attack. The Russian naval commander in San Francisco commented that he would indeed play this anticipated role. Although he was later reprimanded by his superiors for this grandiose unneutral offer, the Russian fleet's presence did give San Francisco a sense of security that it otherwise would not have had.

In April 1865, the Civil War effectively ended with Robert E. Lee's surrender to Ulysses S. Grant in Virginia. Thereupon, construction of the Central Pacific began in earnest. Rolling stock and iron increasingly could be acquired at reasonable cost. By that time the managers of the Central Pacific had also arranged for sufficient labor to do the treacherous work of blasting through the rugged Sierra Nevada on their march eastward.

While the United States then suffered its own domestic turmoil, Chinese conditions were even worse. The specter of starvation forced Chinese workers to sell themselves into virtual slavery just to survive. The Central Pacific purchased "contract labor" in China, brought Chinese workers to California, where they died by the scores in dangerous work blasting a path through the mountains. Few white workers could be persuaded to do such labor. And so, the Chinese built the Central Pacific.

With the war ended, San Francisco financiers found the Central Pacific an attractive investment for the first time. With normal trade resuming, San Francisco's infant industries struggled to compete against goods brought in by sea. In this changing economic environment, San Francisco-based factories no longer lured venture capital.

By contrast, the federal government's doubling of the land grant and the shift in status of the federal loan to a second mortgage made the Central Pacific relatively more appealing. As private money began to become available, progress on the railroad moved rapidly ahead. Soon the Central Pacific and Union Pacific were consumed in a mad race across the continent that captured the imagination of those celebrating a new Union bound together with ribbons of iron.

In this post-war environment, San Francisco manufacturers struggled but held to the hope that the new transcontinental railroad, once finished, might prove to be their salvation. The managers of the Central Pacific promised local manufacturers that they would structure rates on their half of the line to discriminate in favor of San Francisco-made merchandise in the inland domain served by the road. They hinted that eastern-made products would be held to high rates. Cheap eastern goods would necessarily fill boxcars travelling from east to west. But the Central Pacific's only hope to fill boxcars moving from west to east was to give lower rates to San Francisco's products. This logic captured the new manufacturers' collective imagination, as San Franciscans began to envision a commercial empire being carved out for their city with each mile advanced in the eastward march of the Central Pacific.

Likewise, San Franciscans celebrated Columbus's ancient dream of capturing the trade of the Orient that was promised with the completion of the line. Goods from China and Japan shipped by sea to San Francisco could be transshipped by railroad across the North American continent. For this reason also, talk abounded that San Francisco was soon to be the number two urban center in the new Union, second only to New York. San Francisco newspaperman Henry George, soon to become world famous as an economic philosopher, was then an unabashed booster of San Francisco's coming greatness and suggested that the metropolis might soon surpass even New York City itself.

In the late 1860s, investors began to speculate on the limited real estate at the tip of the San Francisco peninsula. The bubble burst not long after the Central Pacific joined the Union Pacific at Promontory, Utah, on May 10, 1869. In that same year, the Suez Canal was finished. This latter improvement eliminated the long European voyage around the continent of Africa for ships bound to Asia. It proved a more attractive lure for the trade of the Orient than did the first American transcontinental railroad. Cargo from the Far East to

Europe by way of the Suez Canal never had to break bulk in a continuous voyage by sea, whereas that sent over the American railroad had to be handled by draymen at least twice—once on the San Francisco waterfront and a second time on New York's waterfront. This was too great an economic disadvantage to allow the railroad to compete effectively with the new canal. And San Francisco real estate values plummeted.

San Francisco's manufacturers complained that the Central Pacific's discriminatory rate schedule, designed to allow California-made products to compete with those made in the East, did not discriminate enough. By contrast, San Francisco's importers cried that these rates discriminated too much and that they should be lower. Whereas in the years immediately before 1869, all of San Francisco had rallied behind the Central Pacific as the champion of their contradictory dreams, everyone became dissatisfied once the new road became a reality.

Even the leaders of the Central Pacific, popularly known as the Big Four (Leland Stanford, Collis P. Huntington, Mark Hopkins and Charles Crocker) quickly became disillusioned as they learned the costs associated with operating a railroad through the Sierra Nevada and Rocky Mountains. Problems of grade and snow removal drove costs up to unforeseen levels. They knew that as soon as entrepreneurs built a rival line over a more southerly transcontinental route, such as that recommended by Jefferson Davis' Army Corps of Engineers during the 1850s, their own snow-bound line could be driven into bankruptcy. Accordingly, they tried to sell their shares in the Central Pacific, but there were no buyers. In the disillusionment that quickly followed the completion of the first transcontinental line, no capitalist risked buying out the Big Four. And so, the railroad entrepreneurs reluctantly stayed on, managing a railroad that had been built over so terrible a route only because of the exigencies of civil war. In their gloom, they saw that unless they themselves built the first southern transcontinental railroad, they might eventually lose their original investment in the Central Pacific. In part because of their own vulnerability, they began to take the first steps toward developing a long-term monopolistic grasp over the state's transportation resources.

The Central Pacific and Union Pacific join at Promontory, Utah, May 10, 1869.

Another long-term consequence of the completion of the Central Pacific in 1869 involved the Chinese workers on the line. In the official photographs of the workers celebrating the completion at Promontory, no Asian face can be found. Had it been possible simply to erase the Chinese after their labor was no longer needed, most white Californians would have been pleased. But the Chinese had no desire to return to unemployment and starvation in their homeland. And so they stayed, locating primarily in San Francisco and Sacramento, where they created a pool of inexpensive labor. Some leading capitalists, such as William C. Ralston, saw this as a boon and envisioned new factories staffed completely with efficient Chinese workers earning slave wages. With Chinese workers, Ralston reasoned, San Francisco's factories would be able to out compete those of Chicago and St. Louis. White workingmen were threatened by such talk and eventually organized to bar Chinese immigration to their state. The Old Union had been rent by issues surrounding African slavery. But in the California of the New Union, it increasingly appeared that Chinese contract labor would soon become a major issue threatening a similar if not equal social and political upheaval.

Suggestions for Further Reading

1, Gerald Stanley, "The Slavery Issue and Election in California, 1860," *Mid-America*, 62 (January 1980), 35-46.

2. Gerald Stanley, "Civil War Politics in California," *Southern California Quarterly*, 64 (Summer 1982), 115-32.

3. Ronald C. Woolsey, "The Politics of a Lost Cause: 'Seceshers' and Democrats in Southern California During the Civil War," *California History*, 69 (Winter 1990/91), 372-83.

4. Oscar Lewis, *The War in the Far West* (1961).

5. John W. Robinson, *Los Angeles in the Civil War* (1977).

6. Leo P. Kibby, "Some Aspects of California's Military Problems During the Civil War," *Civil War History*, 5 (Sept.1959), 251-62.

7. Ward McAfee, *California's Railroad Era, 1850-1911* (1973).

8. Norman E. Tutorow, *Leland Stanford: Man of Many Careers* (1970).

9. Paul M. Ong, "The Central Pacific Railroad and Exploitation of Chinese Labor," *Journal of Ethnic Studies*, 13 (Summer 1985), 119-24.

10. Robert W. Cherny, "City Commercial, City Beautiful, City Practical, The San Francisco Visions of William C. Ralston, James D. Phelan, and Michael M. O'Shaugnessy," *California History*, 73 (Winter 1994/95), 297-307.

11. Ronald C. Woolsey, "Rites of Passage? Anglo and Mexican-American Contracts in a Time of Change: Los Angeles, 1860-1870," *Southern California Quarterly*, 69 (Summer, 1987), 81-102.

VIII
PROGRESS AND POVERTY

The decade of the 1870s began with signs of tremendous progress. The recent completion of the first transcontinental railroad evidenced a new Union, marked by enterprising projects of every sort. San Francisco's William Ralston was building his Bank of California into the leading financial institution in the West. From this position of influence, he orchestrated the industrial growth of San Francisco whose dreams of becoming a Western version of New York were still very much alive. The Central Pacific's Big Four were beginning to consider building another road down into southern California and eastward toward New Orleans. As the decade dawned, it appeared that the age of the entrepreneur was at hand.

But other signs were less positive. Americans began to appreciate increasingly that their past habit of clearing Native Americans away from the path of "progress" was consciously becoming a policy of genocide. This was particularly clear in California, where the earlier Gold Rush had encouraged countless acts of barbarism and abuse against native peoples. Not all Native Americans went peaceably to the reservations set aside on inferior lands. Kientepoos (A.K.A. "Captain Jack") led his Modoc tribe in a furious last stand against white encroachment. Holed up among the lava beds on the south shore of Tule Lake in Siskiyou County in 1873, Captain Jack killed an American general who came into his camp under a flag of truce. This event further enflamed white public opinion and led to the army's subsequent capture and execution of Captain Jack. Defeated and corralled on a reservation, the Modocs continued to diminish in number. It was a pattern that was becoming familiar in American civilization.

Native peoples who lived only with the purpose of preserving and continuing timeless cultures had no place in a society devoted to rapid change and "progress." The Californios were far more like their norteamericano conquerors than were the Indians, but they too could not endure the furious pace of Anglo-American life. American squatters on their land could not understand how any Californio owner deserved so much of Nature's treasure. Not infrequently, this attitude led to altercations and bloodshed, with Californio owners usually getting the worst of the exchange. Together with repeated floods and droughts destroying Californio herds, these culture clashes persuaded some Californios to retreat into Mexico. Others stayed and gradually slid into a degrading poverty during their declining years.

Captured Modoc Indians ("Captain Jack" is shown on

the left with accomplices "Black Jim" and "Boston Charlie") awaiting their execution. Courtesy, Huntington Library.

Especially in California, a simultaneous increase in both progress and poverty characterized the advance of American civilization. Material progress was distributed unevenly, impoverishing those who failed in entrepreneurial, risk-taking adventures. Those who declined to enter the American game of taking such high-stake chances usually sunk into poverty as well. California's business environment often rewarded the rich and punished the poor, yet not even the richest of Californians were guaranteed success. It was a time of "survival of the fittest." Charles Darwin's biological theories were then achieving wide popularity, as Herbert Spencer's translation of them into a sociology of progress at great human expense acquired an aura of true social science. Fortunes were made and lost in an instant. The entrepreneurs who oversaw the construction of the Central Pacific knew this game well. While they built their mansions upon San Francisco's exclusive Nob Hill, they worried incessantly about the ruin that awaited them if they did not succeed in building the first southern transcontinental line. The inherent weaknesses of their Central Pacific necessitated their control of any competing line constructed along a southern route skirting the mountains. They knew that they had to be the fittest to survive.

As the Big Four themselves felt extremely vulnerable, they had little compunction about making others feel even greater anxiety. Burdened with the extraordinary costs of constructing snow sheds over their tracks in the high Sierra, they were constantly seeking ways to make their operations more efficient and economical. Maintaining their railroad's winding entrance to San Francisco Bay down the east bay to San Jose and then up the peninsula to the wharves of San Francisco was too costly. Accordingly, they experimented by building a long wharf out from the shallow waters at Oakland on the east bay to a point of depth that could receive ocean-going vessels. But this experiment floundered due to scouring tides and a wood-eating mollusk that over time undermined the stability of the wharf. Next they settled on a scheme to build a rock bridge out to Goat Island (also called Yerba Buena Island) in the middle of San Francisco Bay. There, they proposed to erect a rival waterfront to San Francisco itself.

The city's leading businessmen organized furiously to block this plan, which threatened to ruin all those who had invested in San Francisco's future. The federal government owned the island and in 1872 bowed to the San Franciscans' pressure not to lease or sell it to the Big Four. "I am losing my grip," wrote Collis P. Huntington, the Central Pacific's principal lobbyist in Washington, D.C. Yet he pressed on even after this failure, for he was ever aware of the fine line between enormous wealth, power and influence on the one hand, and ultimate defeat on the other. Fear of the latter pursued him.

The Panic of 1873, a financial upheaval that left the stock market shaken, undermined business confidence nationally and introduced the depression of the seventies. Today, the federal government works to avoid the destructive whiplash cycles of boom and bust. The Federal Reserve Board regulates the currency and the processes of lending money to venture capitalists. The federal Securities Exchange

Commission regulates the stock market to keep speculation in check. Thus, modern economic competition is moderated by government. In the 1870s, none of these federal regulations of economic activity was in place. The worst economic depression in the nation's history up to that time followed the Panic of 1873, that itself had been preceded by an orgy of railroad speculation and industrial overexpansion.

Hard times hit California. In 1875, William C. Ralston, San Francisco's leading banker and manufacturer, went bankrupt, closing the doors of his Bank of California. His overspeculation in the Comstock silver mines in Nevada contributed most directly to his downfall. Ralston had been a leader of San Francisco's elegant society that aspired to the finest in Europe's epicurean tradition. He had known fantastic wealth. Suddenly, he knew financial ruin as well. Having crossed the thin line separating progress and poverty, he lost all reason for living. Given to taking long swims in San Francisco Bay, Ralston drew no special attention when he entered its frigid waters soon after his financial collapse. When his body was subsequently found, suicide was assumed.

While anxiety plagued the elite during the depression of the 1870s, real hardship was most evident among the working classes of San Francisco and other major California communities. The economic downturn left urban workingmen unemployed or underemployed. In addition, increasing mechanization was changing the very nature of work for the common person. In the past, a workingman had a trade that he had learned as an apprentice, but those trades were fast becoming obsolete. The artistic quality of workmanship was disappearing and being replaced by a lifeless production that was more efficient but personally less fulfilling. Both increasing unemployment and a growing alienation fed a labor upheaval that burned into the soul of urban California during the latter half of the decade.

Denis Kearney, an Irish immigrant, led a working-class rebellion centered in San Francisco in the late 1870s. Night after night, this charismatic orator held outdoor audiences spellbound. His villains varied—the Big Four as symbols of monopolistic greed, and Chinese and prison workers as symbols of unfair competition for the Irish and German immigrant workers that he represented. The Chinese, used to hardships beyond the imaginations of most Californians, offered their labor for wages that those of European origin spurned. Kearney portrayed the Chinese as little different than slaves. The threatened expansion of American Negro slavery into the West had terrorized free white labor before the Civil War destroyed that "peculiar institution." Chinese labor now came to take its place in the white mind in California. "The Chinese must go," shouted Kearney. He painted a picture of hoards of desperate Orientals flooding California's labor markets if determined efforts were not made to cut off their entry.

Similarly, Kearney attacked prison labor as a modern form of slave labor, undermining the economic well being of free workingmen. The idea of San Quentin prisoners contracted out to private entrepreneurs to run machines in factories was especially fearsome. Prison authorities argued that such contracted labor helped defray the costs of maintaining the prison, but Kearney's workingmen could only appreciate the threat convict workers made to their own livelihoods.

In 1877, Kearney became president of the Workingmen's Party of California, challenging the traditional two party system to kneel to his issues. That same year, the Great Railroad Strike in the states of the East and Midwest inspired San Francisco's radicals to increase their agitation. It was Kearney's good fortune that a state constitutional convention had been called to write a new fundamental law for California just as his influence peaked. In 1878, the convention met at Sacramento. One-third of its delegates were Workingmen's Party members, who set the tone of the proceedings by playing the two major parties off of one another. Among key provisions written into the new state constitution were the following: 1) a new state Railroad Commission, with the power to set rates; 2) prohibition against contracting prison labor to private entrepreneurs; and 3) banning of any future Chinese immigration into the state and prohibition of either corporations or governmental agencies hiring Chinese workers already on the scene.

While the new constitution was ratified the following year, each of these provisions was eventually undermined. The Railroad Commission fell prey to the Big Four "investing" in a corrupt Workingmen's candidate for Railroad Commissioner, who joined with the one member out of the three elected who was openly friendly toward the Central Pacific. In this way, the new commission became immediately ineffective. The prohibition against contracted prison labor proved itself to be an empty victory as state authorities simply established state-run prison industries behind prison walls. Eventually, however, meaningful labor in prisons ended because of continuing complaints of free workingmen. As for the Chinese provisions in the new state constitution, they were in violation of the Constitution of the United States and therefore null and void.

Nevertheless, the Workingmen-dominated constitutional convention was not without historical effect. White California's extreme anger against the Chinese persuaded Congress to outlaw any future Chinese immigration in 1882. Four years later, the Statue of Liberty was erected in New York harbor welcoming Europe's poor to seek refuge in the United States. No comparable statue was contemplated for San Francisco, whose white citizens had loudly announced that Asia's impoverished millions should stay at home. The banning of the Chinese constituted the first ethnic restriction of immigration in U.S. history. This proscription continued until World War II.

Throughout the 1870s, the growing white Californian hatred of the Chinese proved significant in another way. Southerners, seeking to call a halt to the federal experiment to "reconstruct" relationships between whites and former African-American slaves, pointed to the seeming national acceptability of Californians openly discriminating against the Chinese. In California, Chinese children were barred from the state's public schools without any corrective action by the federal government. In most Southern states, at least separate schools were provided for black children, at the insistence of Reconstruction Congresses. While by no means a major factor in the termination of Reconstruction in 1877, California's blatant prejudice against the Chinese contributed to making Southern animus against African Americans more politically acceptable.

While Kearney and his cohorts were focusing upon the Chinese, the Big Four were waging their own struggle for survival. Intent upon building the first southern transcontinental line, they acquired the Southern Pacific, a paper corporation with a federal subsidy to build along the southern route. Their rival was Tom Scott, an eastern railroad entrepreneur who controlled the Texas Pacific. The latter company had come into existence too late to get the subsidies that were lavished on firms before the Panic of 1873 weakened the federal treasury. The earlier Credit Mobilier scandal, which involved misuse of subsidy money in the Union Pacific's construction, also contributed to a growing anti-subsidy mood.

Without any subsidies, Scott was at a tremendous disadvantage with the Southern Pacific. Nevertheless, he operated a skilled lobbying machine in Congress; and in the winter of 1876-77, during the political crisis following Rutherford B. Hayes disputed election to the presidency, Scott tried to manipulate Hayes' supporters into backing a federal subsidy for the Texas Pacific as his price for supporting Hayes. Historian C. Vann Woodward has claimed that Scott's men were at the center of the so-called Compromise of 1877 that resulted in Hayes' inauguration, but there are many doubters among professional historians, who question the lack of hard evidence of any commitment by Hayes to any understanding. In any case, Scott never did get a subsidy, and after Hayes' inauguration Scott's dream of beating the Southern Pacific effectively ended.

While Scott was trying to finagle a federal subsidy, the Big Four collected local California subsidies from cities and counties as their construction crews moved southward. Principal of these was a substantial sum granted by Los Angeles to persuade the Southern Pacific to change its originally intended route into southern California by way of the Cajon Pass and San Bernardino. This later proved to be Los Angeles' first major step toward greatness. Rising from southern California's ruin of the 1860s, a new Los Angeles with an entrepreneurial vision of its future succeeded in diverting the Southern Pacific southwestward from its originally intended course into its city limits.

Subsequently building eastward from Los Angeles, the company ran into a less friendly mood in San Bernardino, a town that the Southern Pacific had initially intended to go through upon leaving the San Joaquin Valley. Moving east from Los Angeles (instead of coming south through the Cajon Pass as originally planned), the Southern Pacific asked the proud community for a local subsidy, which was indignantly refused. Thereupon, the company coldly informed San Bernardino that it would bypass the town on its march toward the Colorado River, which was reached in May 1877. San Bernardino languished. By then, Scott was also beaten. Without federal assistance, he made no progress. In 1878, a paralytic stroke incapacitated him, but he hung on to life until 1881. Meanwhile, the Southern Pacific moved steadily ahead and reached New Orleans and the ocean in early 1883, finishing the first southern transcontinental line. With this act, the Big Four guaranteed that their Central Pacific could not be driven into bankruptcy. All the while, they tightened their California monopoly.

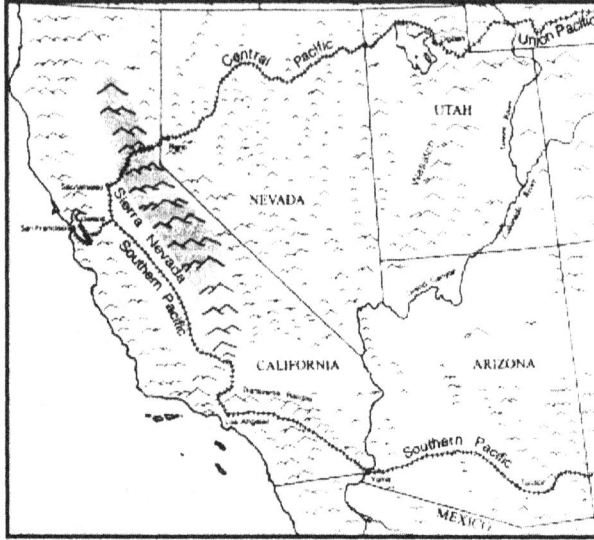

The Big Four's Transcontinental Lines (The shaded area represents the
Sierra Nevada mountains)

By the end of the 1870s, prosperity began to return to both
state and nation, and the worst economic depression to date became
an ugly memory. Had anything been learned from the experience?
San Francisco newspaperman Henry George thought so. During the
seventies, he became the economic philosopher of the Workingmen's
Party. He observed that in San Francisco, the private ownership of
land resulted in the impoverishment of the masses as the city grew.
As progress lured more and more people into San Francisco, real estate values outstripped the ability of common people to purchase land.
As a result, poor people paid inordinate rents to landlords, who in
George's eyes did not deserve wealth that their own labor had not
created. San Francisco's rising land values, George emphasized, had
been created solely by the city's growing population. Accordingly, he
wrote, rents on unimproved land justly belonged to the people as a
whole. To retrieve the increased value of the land for the people,
George proposed a Single Tax—a massive tax on unimproved land to
take from the landowners the unearned increment that they did not
deserve. George promised that proceeds from the Single Tax would
allow all other taxes to be abolished, thus freeing the common person
of all tax burdens. It was a popular notion among workingmen.

In 1879, George published his ideas in a volume entitled *Progress and Poverty*. Instantly, it became an international best seller, and George himself became a leading socialist voice, especially in the English-speaking world. George passionately believed that he had discovered the root cause of the link between progress and poverty. In his eyes, California history revealed it over and again. The Californios had come to control the land before the Gold Rush dramatically increased California's population. Subsequently, state taxation of their real estate at exorbitant rates forced them either to put their land into productive use or surrender it for nonpayment of taxes. This was thoroughly justified in George's eyes. Railroad barons, such as the Big Four, had also acquired imperial domains of real estate through federal grants. Through their control of land surrounding their tracks, they reaped an unfair share of the benefits resulting from their publicly subsidized projects. In George's view, with this unearned increment, the Big Four could bribe Railroad Commissions and evade public regulation. They could rule as potentates in a land supposedly devoted to democratic governance.

The Workingmen's Party of the 1870s attempted to regulate the railroad monopoly, which was dubbed the "Octopus" because of its tentacle-like grip on the economy of the state. In the end, the Workingmen failed to weaken the Big Four. Instead, they effectively diverted public anger and abuse to the Chinese, whom the railroad had brought to the United States as cheap labor. Meanwhile, the "Octopus" appeared always to grow in power and influence. But the railroad's "monopoly" was not perfect. The following decades were to show that it too could be victimized by progress.

Suggestions for Further Reading

1. Henry George, "What the Railroad Will Bring Us," *Overland Monthly*, 1 (Oct. 1868), 297-306.

2. James J. Rawls, *Indians of California* (1984).

3. Gregory A. Reed, *An Historical Geography Analysis of the Modoc Indian War* (1991).

4. David Lavender, *Nothing Seemed Impossible: William C. Ralston and Early San Francisco* (1975).

5. Stuart Daggett, *Chapters on the History of the Southern Pacific* (1922).

6. Lewis B. Lesley, "A Southern Transcontinental Railroad into California: Texas and Pacific Versus Southern Pacific, 1865-1885," *Pacific Historical Review*, 5 (Winter 1936), 52-60.

7. Neil Larry Shumsky, *The Evolution of Political Protest and the Workingmen's Party of California* (1992).

8. Steven J. Ross, "The Culture of Political Economy: Henry George and the American Working Class," *Southern California Quarterly*, 65 (Summer 1983), 145-66.

9. Cheryl L. Cole, "Chinese Exclusion: The Capitalist Perspective of the *Sacramento Union*, 1850-1882," *California History*, 57 (Spring 1978), 8-31.

10. David L. Anderson, "The Diplomacy of Discrimination: Chinese Exclusion, 1876-1882," *California History*, 57 (Spring 1978), 32-45.

11. Ward M. McAfee, "A History of Convict Labor in California," *Southern California Quarterly*, 72 (Spring 1990), 19-40.

IX
THE AGE OF THE "OCTOPUS"

Some modern historians have complained that the popular portrait of an all-powerful railroad monopoly dominating California during the last two decades of the nineteenth century is overdrawn. Nonetheless, their revisionism cannot deny the fact that the so-called "Octopus" was the most important corporation in the state at that time. As railroads were the Pacific coast's most modern and reliable link with the outside world, they were central to the state's economic development. Because the managers of the Southern Pacific had gained an effective monopoly of that resource, economic power was concentrated as in no other time of the state's history. And, as in other times, economic power readily translated itself into political influence.

From 1880 to 1900, the Southern Pacific did not dictate the state's history, but it did help shape it more than any other factor. For this reason, the company acquired the deserved title of "the Octopus," a living organism with tentacles reaching everywhere. The company controlled the state's industrial and agricultural development. Regarding the former, freight rates charged by the company determined the extent to which locally manufactured items could compete with less expensive Midwestern imports. In this sense, the company's rate structure served in a manner similar to protective tariffs on the international level. High tariff rates on foreign goods then gave an artificial advantage to domestic manufacturers. High freight rates on products from Chicago or St. Louis allowed San Francisco-made items to be sold throughout the railroad empire of the Big Four.

The Southern Pacific used rebates to perfect their monopoly over transportation. In 1878, the company inaugurated a "Special Contract System," which granted generous rebates to those shippers who agreed to ship all of their business over their lines. The Special Contract System was designed to strangle ocean-going competition (which offered inexpensive rates for shippers not in a rush to deliver their goods to market) and kept rates high for wheat farmers and others who relied upon both rail and ocean-going vessels to ship their produce.

In the 1880s, California agriculture was dominated by wheat. With the decline of gold fever, some Californians had turned to farming and especially to growing wheat. The interior Sacramento

and San Joaquin valleys were ideally suited for this crop. Mechanization, which allowed rapid expansion of farming in California's broad
and long arable interior valleys in the 1860s, made the state the nation's leading wheat producer in the following decade. In 1880, Hugh
James Glenn, a transplanted Missouri dentist, harvested a half million
bushels on his 55,000 acre ranch in the Sacramento Valley. Known as
the "Wheat King," Glenn was honored by having his domain become
Glenn County in 1891—a political reflection of his ranch's economic
importance. But the preeminence of wheat did not last as the Southern Pacific wished California's agriculture to develop in other directions.

Wheat was carried by rail only as far as ocean-going vessels,
where it was reloaded and shipped to Europe and other points around
the globe. As such, wheat gave only a short haul to the railroad company, which was far more interested in highly perishable fruits and
vegetables that had to be sped eastward quickly, entirely by rail. Railroad magnates viewed southern California's experiments in extensive
orange groves with much greater favor than the great inland valleys'
devotion to wheat.

The Southern Pacific's transportation of citrus fruit eastward
impacted rates elsewhere in California. Initially, the Big Four had
worked to discriminate in favor of western manufactures vis-a-vis
eastern manufactures. These rate structures had not been viewed fa-
vorably by eastern connecting lines, which in turn wanted the lowest
possible rates for eastern manufactured goods moving westward in
order to maximize their own long-haul profits. With the rise of citrus
agriculture in southern California in the 1880s, eastern railroads saw
their opportunity, as they forced a change in the Southern Pacific's
rate structure by agreeing to low rates for perishable oranges only in
exchange for lower rates for eastern goods travelling westward on the
Big Four's lines. In order for southern California's citrus empire to
arise, San Francisco's commercial empire had to shrink, as travelling
salesmen from St. Louis and Chicago encroached upon the economic
boundaries of the bay city.

Droughts in Russia and Argentina brought temporary riches
to California's wheat producers. Likewise, bumper crops in those far-
away places could bring ruin to marginal wheat growers in the state.
Whiplashed in a global agricultural economy, California's wheat
growers looked for some easily understood cause for their frustration
and anxiety. And they found it in the Southern Pacific, which in the

1880s became the official name for all of the Big Four's holdings, including the Central Pacific. Angry farmers and manufacturers simply called it the "Octopus," which they envisioned was strangling the economy of the state.

The public venom poured upon the Octopus was often sim-

THE CURSE OF CALIFORNIA.

plistic. No one could control market forces, not even the Big Four, who did (however) make valiant attempts to manipulate them to the largest degree possible. The Southern Pacific enjoyed the advantage of having more economic and political weapons at its disposal than others. While it was not all-powerful as many envisioned it to be at the time, it was by no means just another player in the game of free-market capitalism.

Naively, the critics of the "Octopus" tried to control it by means of a state railroad commission. Their naiveté was not indicated by their reliance upon governmental regulation, per se. Nor was it necessarily revealed by the fact that the Southern Pacific obviously corrupted a crucial swing vote on the first commission elected following the ratification of the new state constitution in 1879. Rather, their naiveté was exhibited by the fact that the Southern Pacific was a company operating primarily in a national economy. Accordingly, its affairs could not be equitably regulated by a state agency. This realization was slow in coming, as state after state created railroad commissions to regulate rates affecting interstate long-haul rates. Congress took a small step toward erecting a national railroad commission in 1887, when it created the Interstate Commerce Commission. However, this new federal agency was toothless until 1906, when it finally acquired the power to set rates. By contrast, California's Railroad Commission theoretically possessed that power beginning in 1880. In effect, the California commission had the power to disrupt the Southern Pacific's complex inter-regional operations by altering its freight-rate schedule. And so, the railroad corporation focused its energies on keeping the California commission under its control.

Ever changing market forces, not political solutions, provided short-term relief for the Southern Pacific's critics. In 1885, the Atchison, Topeka and Santa Fe railroad completed a second southern transcontinental line. And competition with the Big Four's new Southern Pacific commenced. Both corporations saturated the Midwest with promotional literature on southern California in an attempt to maintain full passenger cars at a time of declining rates. Sick people, the flyers promised, could find restored health in California. As a result of the rate war, sufferers with tuberculosis and a variety of other ailments headed west in what came to be called the "Health Rush" of the late nineteenth century. Overnight, the character of southern California was transformed. While by the 1880s, the Californio Latinos had long been in decline, the Health Rush was to drown their diminishing influence in a sea of midwesterners. New towns multiplied in the greater Los Angeles basin, as the tremendous influx fed real-estate speculation. So many newcomers came that by the early twentieth century Los Angeles was jokingly referred to as "the capital of Iowa." For years thereafter, Angelenos at social gatherings would typically nostalgically recall their Midwestern origins.

The boom in southern California translated into robust business activity throughout the state. As long as it lasted, negative talk against the "Octopus" was minimal as everyone basked in the sunshine of new prosperity. Then, at the end of the eighties the Southern Pacific and its Atchison, Topeka and Santa Fe rival made their first pooling agreement. The two corporations agreed to share profits and effectively not compete. Again, the "Octopus" was in control. Again, the people became restive.

The average Californian was not open to hear discourses on railroad economics and how corporations needed to make a fair return. They knew that these companies had been built with generous public assistance, owned huge landed empires because of federal grants, and that their managers lived in opulence and splendor beyond the imaginations of common folk. Few could empathize with the views of Leland Stanford and Collis P. Huntington, the surviving members of the original Big Four. With the end of the boom of the eighties and the resurrection of anti-railroad feeling, memories of earlier negative events took on greater poignancy. One of these involved the so-called Mussel Slough Massacre of 1880.

The Mussel Slough Massacre had involved a shootout in the San Joaquin Valley between wheat farmers and agents of the Southern Pacific railroad. Land was the source of the conflict. The original Southern Pacific land grant had been to build down the coast. When the corporation shifted its route into the San Joaquin Valley, its right to land in the valley was drawn into question. During the 1870s, before the legal title was resolved, some farmers developed the disputed land with the expectation that when the problem was settled, the railroad would sell it to them at nominal prices. However, these hopes were not realized. Instead, the company offered the land for sale at levels ten to twenty times higher than expected. Accordingly, the farmers organized and resolved to fight for what they regarded as "their land." However, the law was on the side of the legal owner, the railroad company. Ultimately, a gun battle occurred, leaving several farmers dead.

Another incident from the eighties involved the infamous Colton Letters. David D. Colton, a close associate of the Big Four, had died in 1878. His widow subsequently became angered by the Southern Pacific not giving her all that she felt was due from her husband's holdings. Accordingly, in 1883, she took the company to court and embarrassed the Southern Pacific by releasing her deceased husband's correspondence from Collis P. Huntington, the company's chief lobbyist in Washington, D.C. The letters revealed details about Huntington's willingness to corrupt the democratic process. This evidence helped motivate reformers in the early nineties to attempt to bring the "Octopus" under public control.

In the early nineties, frustrated San Francisco businessmen organized the Traffic Association of California to elect a new Railroad Commission to lower rates. Yet, once in office, the new commission wavered. Given the detailed content of the Colton Letters on the political methods of the Southern Pacific, many people suspected corruption. But then the commission dramatically lowered rates affecting grain producers. With the swiftness of a cat, the company appealed the rate changes in the U.S. Circuit Court of Northern California, headed by Judge Joseph McKenna, an old personal friend of Leland Stanford. McKenna immediately ordered an injunction and proceeded to review the facts of the case.

The California constitution forbade appeals of commission rate decisions. Nevertheless, McKenna ruled that the Fourteenth Amendment of the U.S. Constitution took primacy over the state constitution and that the commission's action had unconstitutionally denied the company the possibility of a fair profit. With this result, cynics suspected that the Octopus first corrupted the Railroad Commission, then directed it to lower rates to such an extreme degree that many reasonable people would agree with McKenna's ruling. The entire affair appeared to have been rigged. Thereafter, the California Railroad Commission was not feared by the Southern Pacific.

The onslaught of a national economic depression in 1893 made matters more desperate. This depression was even worse than that of the "terrible seventies" and served to radicalize workers once again. During the bloody Pullman Strike of 1894, which involved rail lines nationwide, strikers seized Oakland's railroad yards and openly challenged public authorities. Middle-class California, while initially sympathetic to the workers, could not abide the specter of class warfare and revolution. Opposed by both the federal and state governments, the strike ultimately collapsed. In California, it appeared that once again the Octopus had triumphed.

Meanwhile, the Traffic Association of California made one last attempt to curb the power of the Southern Pacific. Under the leadership of Claus Spreckles, who had come penniless from his native Germany to become the state's sugar-beet king, the Traffic Association built the San Francisco and San Joaquin Valley Railway down the valley and in 1898 reached Bakersfield. A year later, Spreckles shocked the Traffic Association by selling the line to the Atchison, Topeka and the Santa Fe, giving it a connection into the Bay Area. He justified his action by claiming that some competition between the Santa Fe's Valley Road and the Southern Pacific had to occur, the record of past pooling agreements notwithstanding. The unexpected sale left San Franciscans devastated.

While gloom enveloped San Francisco at the end of the century, the mood in Los Angeles was more upbeat. Los Angeles was on its way toward becoming the leading city of the West. It too warred with the Southern Pacific but with a happier conclusion. The conflict involved the location of Los Angeles's improved harbor facilities. The Los Angeles Chamber of Commerce wanted San Pedro selected as the harbor that was to be enlarged by the construction of a man-made breakwater at federal expense. Having acquired railroad facilities in the 1870s, Los Angeles in the 1890s was planning a world-class port, capable of rivaling San Francisco's natural harbor. However, Collis P. Huntington wanted the site for the federal breakwater to be Santa Monica, where his Southern Pacific controlled most of the surrounding real estate. The battle raged throughout the nineties, but by the end of the decade the city fathers won by persistently exposing Huntington's underhanded lobbying efforts. The victory was especially uplifting, not only because it projected the future greatness of Los Angeles, but also for demonstrating that the Octopus did not always win. Goliath could be conquered.

Young William Randolph Hearst also revealed the Octopus' vulnerability. Inheriting millions from his Nevada-silver-king father, young Hearst made his mark as publisher of the *San Francisco Examiner* and other newspapers from coast to coast. He experimented with a new type of reporting, known as "yellow journalism." At its best, it involved careful research and passionate story writing about public ills. At its worst, it was characterized by blatant sensationalism and (if it was needed to sell newspapers) outright lies. Hearst's role in pushing the nation into the Spanish-American War of 1898 contained many examples of yellow journalism at its worst. Hearst's exposé of the Southern Pacific's efforts to avoid repaying sums loaned by the federal government to the Central Pacific in the 1860s exemplified a better aspect of his new style of journalism.

In the 1890s, Hearst mounted a campaign of publicity revealing how Huntington was trying to manipulate Congress into refunding the Central Pacific's federal loan so that the company effectively would never have to pay it back. His ultimate success revealed to that generation that even the best financed lobbyist scheme could not withstand the glare of publicity in a land that still called itself a democracy. By the end of the nineties, even the crusty Huntington had to admit defeat, and the old loan began to be paid off, leaving only the land grants as a free gift from the public. Similar to the "Free Harbor Fight" of Los Angeles, Hearst's victory over the Southern Pacific concerning the Funding Bill proved that the Octopus was not invincible.

Nevertheless, these victories did not persuade Californians that they should relax their guard against the Southern Pacific. There were many important battles yet to be fought. Reformers perceived that the company actively contributed to a growing corruption of the democratic process. In the late nineteenth century, San Francisco was especially susceptible to corporate interests purchasing votes. In those days, recent immigrants could vote even before becoming citizens. Peoples from eastern and southern Europe characterized the so-called New Immigration which came to San Francisco. As early as 1889, *The Overland Monthly*, commented, "With a population more than half foreign, with more saloons and open vice of every sort--so the students of such things tell us—than any other city in the Union, San Francisco is building up a hoodlumism that may yet prove terrific. In our shiftless, discouraged Polish Jews, Irish or Italians, there is the making of a slum population bad as in any city."

At that time, there was no governmental welfare system to meet the needs of the dislocated and dispossessed. There were no government social workers to meet the needs of unemployed persons. However, there were private welfare services organized by big-city political bosses, who were most influential in places like San Francisco. These political entrepreneurs took advantage of both the New Immigrant's extreme poverty and his lack of experience in democratic processes. The boss, or his ward healers (district representatives who commonly spoke the various languages of the immigrants), could get an errant son out of jail, or temporarily put food on the table, or even find a match for an older daughter. All that was asked in return was a vote, delivered at the polls openly as the boss required. Reformers tried to curb this practice by enactment of a statewide "Australian" secret ballot law in 1891, but it was ineffective. The boss continued to wield unusual influence at the state nominating conventions of the two major parties, where he was eager to sell his urban votes to the highest bidder. As the dominant economic power in the state, the Southern Pacific had the ability to win this bidding contest and block the nomination of any troublemakers arising in either party.

By the end of the century, a new generation was coming of age. In California and elsewhere, this generation was intent to save the best from the past while adjusting to an economy more dynamic, complex and interdependent than ever before. As state and nation pulled out of depression at the close of the century, civic-minded reformers resolved to reinvent American democracy, so that monopolies could exercise neither undue political nor economic influence. Despairing over the ugly underside of changing economic conditions, they cherished a hope that all might yet be well, as they focused upon the Octopus as the symbol of all that was wrong with California society.

Suggestions for Further Reading

1. William Deverell, *Railroad Crossing, California and the Railroad, 1850-1910* (1994).

2. Gloria Ricci Lathrop, "The Boom of the '80s Revisited," *Southern California Quarterly*, 75 (Fall/Winter, 1993), 263-301.

3. Leonard Pitt, *The Decline of the Californios* (1966).

4. Richard J. Orsi, "The Octopus Reconsidered: The Southern Pacific and Agricultural Modernization in California, 1865-1915," *California Historical Quarterly*, 54 (Fall 1975), 197-220.

5. For the growth of citrus agriculture in southern California, see the entire issue of *California History*, 74 (Spring 1995).

6. John A. Larimore, "Legal Questions Arising From the Mussel Slough Land Dispute," *Southern California Quarterly*, 58 (Spring 1976), 75-94.

7. Ward M. McAfee, "A Constitutional History of Railroad Rate Regulation in California, 1879-1911," *Pacific Historical Review*, 37 (August 1968), 265-79.

8. Louis A. DiDonato, "The Great Railroad Strike of 1894 in Southern California," *Southern California Quarterly*, 76 (Spring 1996), 153-74.

9. William A. Bullough, *The Blind Boss and His City: Christopher Augustine Buckley and Nineteenth Century San Francisco* (1979).

10. Eric Falk Petersen, "The Struggle for the Australian Ballot in California," *California Historical Quarterly*, 51 (Fall 1972), 227-43.

11. Curtis E. Grassman, "Prologue to California Reform: The Democratic Impulse, 1886-1898," *Pacific Historical Review*, 42 (Nov. 1973), 518-36.

13. Kevin Starr, *Americans and the California Dream, 1850-1915* (1973).

X

THE CALIFORNIA MIND AT THE TURN OF THE CENTURY

At the turn of the century, California was a divided society. The very rich lived in spacious mansions. The very poor fared miserably in the kind of crowded slums that existed south of San Francisco's Market Street. There were no governmental provisions for those who failed to provide for themselves. There were no effective governmental regulations to curb the extraordinary economic power of large corporations, such as the Southern Pacific. Some justified these conditions by claiming that free market capitalism alone could produce progress. This was the message of Social Darwinism. Ironically, many of those who trumpeted such notions interfered with free market forces whenever it suited their purposes. For example, in the 1880s, both major political parties cooperated in banning Chinese immigration on the grounds that it contributed to unfair economic competition. This interfered with free market forces. In the 1890s, the Republican party advocated high federal protective tariffs to keep foreign products from competing in the American economy. And not only politicians interfered with the operations of the free market: The Southern Pacific, the Santa Fe and other railroad corporations entered into pooling agreements to stifle competition, whether or not the fittest survived under such circumstances.

In their handling of the Chinese issue, Californians revealed the shallow quality of their belief in "survival of the fittest." Social Darwinist Josiah Strong had argued in *Our Country* (1885) that with the passing of the American frontier a final competition among the races was soon to commence in Asia, the supposed next frontier for Anglo-Americans. Yet competition with the Chinese had been denied in California out of fear that Asians might win this cultural contest. If the game could not be won in California, how could victory be achieved in the Far East?

Though not a Californian, Strong did much to shape the California mind at the turn of the century. His cry for a revised Manifest Destiny reaching out across the Pacific to a new Asian frontier alerted Californians to the fact that their state was soon to become a center for a new imperialist crusade. Alfred T. Mahan's *The Influence of Sea Power Upon History* (1890) supplemented Strong's vision.

Mahan, an instructor at the U.S. Naval Academy, argued that if the United States hoped to win in any serious competition among nations, it needed a world-class navy capable of dominating in not only the Atlantic but also the Pacific. His vision of superior American naval power in the vast Pacific Ocean captured the public imagination. In order to maximize that power, a Central American canal was needed. Such a canal was certain to promote economic development in California, which inevitably would become a naval center for America's expansion into the Pacific. American acquisitions in the Pacific, resulting from the Spanish-American War of 1898, made this vision of California's future all the more firm.

Most Americans then found Social Darwinism to be attractive when projecting a subjection of foreign peoples. Imperialism promised new markets and more economic opportunities. Application of Social Darwinistic assumptions to lower classes within the United States more readily offended popular democratic sensibilities. Nevertheless, domestic social conditions suggested that "survival of the fittest" was already occurring within the United States. The existence of widespread poverty in San Francisco, a glittering jewel of a city enjoyed by a wealthy elite unmatched along the Pacific slope, revealed that not all Americans could win the race for riches and power. In fact, San Francisco's demography suggested that most were destined to lose. This had been the message of Henry George's *Progress and Poverty* (1879).

The fact that extreme poverty existed in San Francisco mocked the popular American notion that the West offered any special opportunity to the common man. "Go West, young man," Horace Greeley had advised an entire generation seeking new opportunities after the Civil War. Many had gone and found only despair in San Francisco. In fact, across America the depression of the 1890s convinced many that the American dream had ended. Historian Frederick Jackson Turner offered his famous essay "The Significance of the Frontier in American History" in 1893, suggesting that the disappearance of the frontier threatened democratic values themselves. Democracy was based upon at least the hope of a relative equality of opportunity shared by all citizens, and that was evaporating. From the time of Columbus to the 400th anniversary of his voyage in 1892, the New World had represented a bonanza of opportunity for the common white man. That boon, Turner gloomily prophesied, was coming to an end. The sociology of turn-of-the-century San Francisco seemed to prove his point.

Early in the new century, more than one Californian elaborated upon this gloom in works of fiction that soon became national classics. One of these was *The Octopus* (1901), Frank Norris's, fictional account of the Mussel Slough Massacre of 1880. His novel portrayed a California in which hard-working farmers were gunned down by the representatives of a railroad corporation that looked very much like the hated Southern Pacific. Yet Norris avoided a simplistic demonization of the railroad monopoly. Near the end of the novel, in a revealing conversation between the fictional counterpart of Collis P. Huntington and the story's hero, Norris communicated that no one was able to stop an increasing global economic interdependence that easily spawned temporary human inequities and social injustice. While Norris ended his book with the pollyannaish idea that Social Darwinism inevitably worked for both progress and ultimately a greater justice, the individual tragedies taking up the bulk of his novel belied any sense of easy optimism. *The Octopus* clearly revealed a darkening of the California mind at the turn of the century.

It was then common knowledge that California harbored many unhappy stories. Helen Hunt Jackson traveled west looking for one of them. A nationally known reformer for Indian rights, she came to California in the 1880s to research what was to become her most famous novel, *Romona*, which was published in 1884. It depicted the destruction of the California Indians following the end of the mission system. Her goal was to awaken consciences in her portrayal of an Anglo-American mauling of Native Americans. But readers fed most upon her romanticization of the mission system, within which paternalistic padres supposedly sheltered their Indian charges from a cruelly free environment just beyond the mission walls. Increasingly pessimistic about their future, Californians and other Americans fixed upon Jackson's portrayal of the placid days of California's Hispanic past as a welcome escape.

In the public imagination, California became associated with a genteel Spanish past, populated by kindly mission fathers and dashing rancheros, as Jackson's *Romona* came to influence the architecture of turn-of-the-century California. The building styles of Spanish California, featuring red-tile roofs and inner courtyards resembling the defunct missions, became the rage. Southern California especially evidenced this new style, but even as far north as the Bay Area, *Ro-*

mona's architectural influence could be seen. Stanford University, founded in 1891 by one of the Big Four on his farm at Palo Alto, was marked by red-tile roofs, long arched walkways, and interior court-yards. In southern California, Riverside's Mission Inn became the epitome of Mission Revival architecture. This style proved popular and advertised California as a vacation land where visitors could come to restore their battered spirits amidst recollections of a lost romantic past.

Stanford University's Inner Quad (left) and Riverside's Mission Inn (right) both re-flected the Mission Revival architectural style.

Despite the unintended architectural impact of *Romona*, Helen Hunt Jackson's life's work of literary lobbying for Native Americans did succeed in spurring Congress to pass the Dawes Sev-eralty Act of 1887. At the time, that act was viewed as a pro-Indian reform, as it allowed individual Indians to acquire reservation land and theoretically become independent yeoman farmers. The act's sponsors blamed the increasing signs of Indian decline upon the res-ervation system, which was credited with fostering indolence and general degradation. Their analysis was shallow. By allowing federal grants of land to individual Indians, the act inevitably shrunk the size of the reservations, and tribal cultures were further weakened in the process. The act was founded on the assumption that Indian redemp-tion could best occur through assimilation into the white man's world, a world then marked by a "survival of the fittest" sociology. In such a harsh environment, individual Indians operating on their own in an alien culture had minimal chances of success.

California's primary individual contributor to the ideology of Social Darwinism was Stephen Field, who had been a member of the California Supreme Court in the 1850s. Field's own rise to prominence occurred in a brutal environment in which only "the fit" could survive. In 1859, California's Chief Justice David Terry had killed California's U.S. Senator David Broderick. Thereupon, Field himself became Chief Justice. Lincoln then promoted Field to the U.S. Supreme Court in 1863. From this position, he articulated the nation's constitutional law for the next generation. His contribution was central, as he became the philosophical leader of the highest court in the land. At first, he publicized his strong Social Darwinist views in dissents; but by the 1890s, his public-policy belief which dictated that government should not interfere with the workings of free market capitalism became characteristic of the court's majority opinions. He used the Fourteenth Amendment, not to protect African Americans from prejudicial state governments (which had been the intent of its framers), but rather to shelter railroad corporations from state regulation. Field reasoned that the Fourteenth Amendment effectively blocked a state from regulating corporations in any way which might threaten them from earning a fair profit. His attentions were devoted to encouraging "the fit," as opposed to protecting those in marginal circumstances. When Field retired in 1897, his place on the nation's highest court was filled by none other than Joseph McKenna, who earlier had proven himself to be an apt student of Field's constitutional theories in gutting the California Railroad Commission.

Field's belief in Social Darwinism was put to the test in an episode involving his own personal safety. In the late 1880s, Field ruled against one Althea Hill, who lost her suit to gain a wife's share of the estate of silver baron William Sharon. Sharon had acquired many of William Ralston's properties after the drowning death of the latter in the 1870s. Hill, who only had been Sharon's mistress, apparently falsified a marriage contract, upon which she rested her case. Ms. Hill's legal counsel was none other than the murderous David Terry, who himself then married Hill and vowed revenge against Field, his former colleague. As Terry already had gotten away with killing one high-ranking federal official with whom he had a disagreement, Field took the threat seriously.

Terry caught up with Field at a restaurant near Stockton, where he struck the first blow. In response, Field's bodyguard gunned Terry down before shocked diners. The episode made complete sense in a world characterized by a brutal struggle for survival. The bodyguard, David Neagle, was subsequently successfully defended in court by one William F. Herrin, who so impressed Collis P. Huntington that Herrin was made the Southern Pacific's chief counsel in 1893, and from that position ran the company's manipulation of state politics well into the twentieth century.

Despite the pervasiveness of the survival-of-the-fittest ideology in California at that time, the state also claimed Luther Burbank, who inspired some of Social Darwinism's leading critics. From his farm in Santa Rosa, Burbank became world famous for tinkering with Mother Nature in hybridizing fruits, flowers and vegetables. The idea behind Burbank's life's work was simple: Because human beings have intelligence, they can improve nature. Unlike animals, who can only live by the law of the jungle, men and women have the capacity to reform, to regulate, to create anew. Burbank described his hybrids in a series of publications between 1893 and 1901. Socialists drew inspiration from his work and claimed that rather than relying upon survival of the fittest, in a competitive free-for-all, far more beneficial results could be had by tinkering with the way society was managed.

So-called Nationalist Clubs, calling for the nationalization of railroad corporations, attracted those of a socialist bent. They thrived in California during the Populist Movement of the 1890s and were the outgrowth of Edward Bellamy's *Looking Backward: 2000-1887* (1888), a popular fantasy of a future socialist society. Bellamy called for a peaceful national conversion to socialism. While neither Bellamy nor Populism originated in California, both helped encourage Californians to consider socialist solutions to California's problems. One of the Populists' principal planks called for the nationalization of railroad corporations. Mere government regulation of railroads had clearly failed in California. The Populist hope was that justice would come with public ownership of transportation giants such as the Southern Pacific.

John Muir exhibited certain socialist tendencies but was more tightly focused than either Bellamy or the Populists. Muir, a Scottish-born fruit grower in the Bay Area, devoted his life to saving a California wilderness that he feared was soon to be obliterated by the march of "progress." Like Bellamy, he believed that the laissez-faire public policies of Social Darwinists could only lead to disaster. But rather than call for a general socialization of the economy, as did Bellamy, Muir sought only to achieve governmental protection for his beloved wilderness. In 1890, Muir succeeded in getting Congress to establish Yosemite Valley as a national park. He had lived there from 1868 to 1874, virtually worshipping the natural splendor all about him. Subsequently, he publicized its wonders in an effort to achieve governmental protection from private interests. He was unwilling to risk this treasure of granite walls and cascading waterfalls to the unregulated world of free market capitalism.

Fresh from this triumph, Muir helped found the Sierra Club in San Francisco in 1892. The stated purpose of this new organization was "to explore, enjoy, and render accessible the mountain regions of the Pacific Coast; to publish authentic information concerning them; to enlist the support and cooperation of the people and the government in preserving the forests and other natural features of the Sierra Nevada." Muir, himself, became the club's first president. He desired first to conserve, ultimately to preserve, that which was wild in an increasingly "developed" landscape. As much as the pronouncements of Frederick Jackson Turner, the creation of the Sierra Club symbolized the ending of the American frontier.

Not only did Muir not want selfish private interests to destroy the wild, he also did not want natural wonders exploited for some "greater" public good. In resisting the latter, he fought a losing cause to save Hetch Hetchy Valley (like Yosemite, a glacial valley of incredible beauty) from being converted into a reservoir to supply San Francisco with water. The fight over Hetch Hetchy, which occurred early in the new century, split the Sierra Club, some of whose members appreciated the societal need of guaranteeing the bay city's on-going water resources. As for Muir, San Francisco's ultimate victory broke his will to live.

Entering a new century, California reflected many intellectual cross-currents. For one, the racism of the new American imperialism, projecting itself out across the Pacific Ocean to the Far East, abounded in California. Chinese immigration had been banned, thus keeping Chinese women from joining their men in California. The largely male Chinese population extant in the golden state was forced to grow old without the benefit of wives and families. As Chinatowns became centers of opium addiction and prostitution, most whites simply chalked this tragedy up to racial inferiority. The ideology of Social Darwinism provided a pseudo-scientific aura for a very old-fashioned white racism.

Imperialistic racism, gloomy pessimism, libertarian independence and a desire to manage society by governmental action—all swirled in a cauldron of seeming contradiction. Typically, California's residents had come to the state in order to maximize their personal liberty. They came to escape the more tightly restricted social mores found in eastern states. Yet few were confident that they would not be crushed in California's laissez-faire economic environment, where a court-protected "fair profit" for the Southern Pacific might eliminate opportunity for a small businessman or struggling farmer. Californians were open to using government to correct perceived societal wrongs, but few were willing to surrender substantial personal freedom in a tightly managed socialist economy, such as envisioned by Edward Bellamy. David Starr Jordan, Stanford University's president between 1891 and 1913, commented upon this aspect of the state's collective personality in an essay that appeared in the *Atlantic Monthly* in 1898:

> The dominant note in the social development of the state is individualism.... Man is man, in California; he exists for his own sake, not as part of a social organism. He is, in a sense, superior to society.... Life on the coast has, for him, something of the joyous irresponsibility of a picnic. The feeling of children released from school remains with grown people.

Californians were unlikely candidates to erect a Bellamy-like regimented utopia. On the other hand, pessimistic about the continuing consequences of an unregulated economy, they were at least willing to talk of moving in the direction of a more "managed" society. This unresolvable tension between love of personal freedom and a desire to increase governmental interference with free-market capitalism came to characterize the Progressive Movement that blossomed early in the new century.

More than any other turn-of-the-century Californian, novelist Jack London perhaps best characterized the contradictions of his time and place. Similar to Frank Norris, who was a close personal friend, he saw a hard, competitive world all about him. Similar to Norris, he appreciated the savage nature of man, covered only by a thin veneer of "civilization." Both were students of Social Darwinism. London had grown up along Oakland's harsh waterfront environment and had participated in the Klondike gold rush to Alaska in 1897-98.

He prided himself on not being naive about the brutal nature of existence.

A rugged individualist, London also proudly defined himself as a socialist. Yet it is hard to imagine so free a spirit ever living comfortably in a tightly regulated society. His was a romantic socialism thriving on passionate rhetoric. He wrote much about his Alaskan experiences, a life characterized by individual adventure, not a desire for a managed social order. *The Call of the Wild* (1903) is perhaps his most widely read book. Part of him was similar to John Muir, a free man in love with the wilderness. Racism and imperialistic nationalism were also part of his make-up. Such was the complexity of the California mind at the turn of the century, on the eve of the Progressive Movement.

Suggestions for Further Reading

1. Sucheng Chan, *Entry Denied: Exclusion and the Chinese Community in America, 1883-1943* (1991).

2. Valerie Sherer Mathes, *Helen Hunt Jackson and Her Indian Reform Legacy* (1990).

3. G. Allen Greb, "Opening a New Frontier: San Francisco, Los Angeles, and the Panama Canal, 1900-1914," *Pacific Historical Review*, 47 (Aug.1978), 405-24.

4. John T. McGreevy, "Farmers, Nationalists, and the Origins of California Populism," *Pacific Historical Review*, 58 (Nov.1989), 471-95.

5. Frank Norris, *The Octopus* (1901).

6. Joseph R. McElrath, *Frank Norris: A Descriptive Biography* (1992).

7. Stoddard Martin, *California Writers: Jack London, John Steinbeck, The Tough Guys* (1983).

8. Roderick W. Nash, *Wilderness and the American Mind* (1967/ 1982).

9. Thurman Wilkins, *John Muir: Apostle of Nature* (1995).

10. Carl B. Swisher, *Stephen J. Field* (1930).

11. David Starr Jordan, *California and the Californians* (1907).

XI
PROGRESSIVE CALIFORNIA

In September 1901, upon William McKinley's assassination, Theodore Roosevelt became the youngest president in American history. The new president, who had captured the public's imagination with his charge up San Juan Hill during the Spanish-American War, embodied the active spirit of his generation. As one who in his twenties had punched cattle in the Dakotas, he keenly felt the passing of the American frontier. As a former police commissioner of New York City and as a former governor of New York state, he was acutely aware of the multi-faceted urban problems facing a post-frontier America. Unlike his predecessor, who represented the past as the nation's last president to have served in the Civil War, Roosevelt eagerly addressed the challenges of the new century. In his own words, he used the presidency as "a bully pulpit" to stir the nation to adjust politically to a new urban industrial order.

Inspired by Roosevelt's leadership, progressives throughout the nation sought to curb the power of corporate elites to dictate major economic decisions to a weak and divided public. In the late nineteenth century, large corporations had proven their ability to manipulate the American economy and corrupt the democratic process. In California, this issue focused upon the state's most powerful corporation, the Southern Pacific. Progressives were also disturbed by big-city political bosses, eager and willing to sell the voting power of the urban poor to the highest corporate bidder. In California, this problem centered upon the political dynamics of San Francisco, burdened with an impoverished immigrant population.

At the turn of the century, San Franciscans grieved the slow erosion of the premier status of their city. In part, San Francisco's diminished growth rate was due to the Southern Pacific. As shown in an earlier chapter, the rise of citrus agriculture in southern California was closely tied to a whittling away of San Francisco's favored status by the Southern Pacific's designers of interstate rate schedules. By contrast, Los Angeles was well situated vis-a-vis several southern transcontinental lines—a geographic advantage which insured lower rates. Nevertheless, Angelenos too were distrustful of the Southern Pacific. They perceived the corporation's desire to harness their city's development by dictating the location of a federal breakwater at Santa

Monica. That the S.P. had failed in this attempt in no way diminished the memory of its latent power.

Progressive Angelenos were not inherently opposed to concentrated wealth shaping the contours of their city, as their easy acceptance of Henry E. Huntington demonstrated. In 1900, Collis P. Huntington died, leaving a substantial portion of his fortune to his nephew, Henry E. Huntington. Thereupon, the younger Huntington exhibited his own entrepreneurial skills in southern California. His mushrooming Pacific Electric interurban rail system throughout the greater Los Angeles basin in the early twentieth century shaped the future of Los Angeles, yet progressives typically did not complain. Most progressives were not socialists. Few of them had any desire to have government dictate economic development. Accordingly, they had no inherent animus toward enterprising capitalists such as Henry E. Huntington, whose expanding interurban rail network provided a desired improvement that propelled Los Angeles' growth toward the state's largest metropolis. For their part, progressive Angelenos only wanted the power to veto any action by concentrated wealth which they felt was against the public interest. They spoke of trusting no one but "the people."

Ironically, the attitude of the Southern Pacific's managers was somewhat similar to that of the progressives—not in trusting "the people," but rather in only desiring a veto voice over their enemies' efforts to control their course. The corporation had no interest in running the politics of the state in any comprehensive way. William F. Herrin's power as the corporation's political overseer was real, but much of the popular mythology regarding him was overblown. Rather than striving for total control, Herrin typically focused his energies surgically to cut, remove, or render harmless individual politicians who threatened the Southern Pacific's economic empire.

From their earliest days in politics, the railroad barons themselves had typically viewed their political involvements as defensive in nature. In the 1870s, when hostile railroad bills were before both houses of the legislature, the Southern Pacific had typically focused its energies on controlling the votes of only ten of forty senators. Any investment in the more numerous state assembly would have proven too expensive. And so they spent little or nothing in that quarter. Normally they could count upon at least ten or eleven of the forty-man Senate to vote with them honestly, out of conviction. That left only ten to manipulate by dishonest methods in order to get a majority of that body needed to block unfriendly legislation. Their modus operendi never changed.

In the 1880s, Collis P. Huntington had become intensely angry with Leland Stanford when the latter allowed himself to be chosen a U.S. Senator by the state legislature. Huntington feared that it would appear that the railroad company was trying to control the politics of the state, which it was not. Thereafter, Huntington effectively stripped Stanford of influence in the corporation's affairs. By 1893, Stanford was dead, and the company was led by Huntington alone, with William Herrin as his political manager. In the 1890s and early in the twentieth century, the Southern Pacific left most of state politics alone, moving in only when it sensed danger.

Progressives also regarded their own strategy as largely defensive in nature. Typically, both nationwide and in California, the progressives did not seek to control the means of production. Unlike the Populists of the 1890s, they did not urge a nationalization of railroads. Typically, they sought only to regulate corporate power by the empowering of state and federal regulatory agencies. Any socialist tendencies were reserved for local politics, where many progressives advocated what some called "gas and water socialism," or public ownership and management of urban gas and water companies.

Los Angeles' John Randolph Haynes was a typical "gas and water socialist" in the progressive ranks. A Christian-socialist millionaire, Dr. Haynes was an advocate of the Social Gospel, or the notion that the salvation offered by Jesus Christ was not intended only for individuals. Modern industrial society had erected a complex economy, capable of both good and evil. Social Gospel advocates such as Haynes argued that Christian teachings commanded that economic and political systems be reformed to insure "social justice." Haynes especially put great faith in the people themselves to bring about an approximation of Christ's Kingdom on earth. Accordingly, he advocated "direct democracy," which involved various mechanisms to allow the people to control their political destinies directly, thereby bypassing any elected representatives who might be tempted by corporate dollars.

The progressive spirit was founded upon a faith in the people to govern themselves. The nation's founding fathers had not been as sanguine about the people's ability divorced from the refining wisdom of elected representatives. The U.S. Constitution itself reflected this earlier understanding. For example, it had provided that the people choose "electors," who in turn would select a president. Likewise, under the original Constitution the people elected state legislatures, which in turn chose U.S. Senators. Haynes believed that he had a better idea, that being to maximize the people's power directly to affect politics. Only in this way, he believed, could the ability of concentrated wealth to corrupt local, state and federal legislative bodies be broken. In 1902, Haynes succeeded in getting Los Angeles to amend its city charter to institute the initiative, referendum and recall on the local level.

The initiative was a means whereby a proposition could be placed on the ballot by gathering a sufficient number of petition signatures. By comparison, the referendum was a mechanism to freeze a bill that had already been passed by a legislative body. By gathering a sufficient number of petition signatures to allow the people themselves to vote on the measure, a referendum was put on the ballot to veto the legislation. Recall was a similar method of placing on the ballot the name of an offensive elected official for possible removal before the end of his regular term. During the Progressive Era, almost half of the states (including California) would enact such mechanisms of "direct democracy."

As Angeleno reformers focused upon direct democracy as their hope for the future, San Francisco progressives exposed the corruption that then typified their city's government. The great San Francisco earthquake of 1906 was a catalyst for their efforts. By tearing open public buildings to reveal a lack of quality in construction, the disaster proved that city building contracts had been rife with fraud. Fremont Older, the editor of the *San Francisco Bulletin*, devoted his energies to uncovering the roots of this corruption, which led directly to Abraham Ruef, the urban political boss behind corrupt elected officials. "'Muckraking" journalism that exposed public scandals was then in style across the nation. Lincoln Steffens, a native San Franciscan, had gained national renown with his series of article-length revelations of municipal corruption that were published in book form in *The Shame of the Cities* (1904). This provided a model for Older's own investigative reporting which led to the trial and conviction of Ruef, who was sent to San Quentin for his crimes.

These local victories encouraged progressives to take their movement statewide. In 1907, they organized the Lincoln-Roosevelt League, a reform caucus within the statewide Republican Party that enjoyed some success in the 1908 legislative elections. The following

year, they won the enactment of a direct primary law in the state legislature. This was a most significant reform, as it junked the old
party-convention method of selecting nominees for high office. In
state conventions, corporate elites and big city bosses had made their
deals. The direct primary law broke this arrangement, putting into the
hands of common voters the power to nominate the leaders of their
parties for important state positions. In the first direct primary, held in
1910, Hiram Johnson won the Republican nomination for governor.
Virtually unknown just a few years earlier, he had gained fame as the
lead prosecutor of Boss Ruef in the trial that sent the latter to jail.
Himself the alienated son of a Southern Pacific machine politician,
Johnson made his election slogan "Kick the Southern Pacific out of
California Politics."

As if to symbolize his independence from the Southern Pacific, Johnson refused to campaign by rail and instead drove a shiny
red automobile from town to town on the state's primitive road system. He was elected governor, and progressives of both parties gained
control of the state legislature. Herrin was defeated. The next year,
under Johnson's direction, the Public Utilities Commission was created to replace the old defunct California Railroad Commission.
Armed with the power to regulate a variety of public utilities (including railroads), the new commission made it appear as if the Southern
Pacific indeed had been kicked out of California politics.

In fact, the California progressives' victory over the "Octopus" involved more symbolism than substance. In 1906, President
Roosevelt had succeeded in getting Congress to enact the Hepburn
Act, which involved a significant overhaul of the Interstate Commerce Commission, the federal agency that had been initially created
in 1887 to investigate railroad operations nationwide For years, the
I.C.C. had been ineffectual. But the Hepburn Act changed this. After
1906, the I.C.C. had the power to set railroad rates throughout the
nation. This was one of the most significant reforms to come out of
Roosevelt's presidency, as it brought order to an interstate railroad
rate system ruled for over a generation by caprice, ruthless corporate
maneuvers and occasional agreements among companies to pool their
profits and not compete with each other.

In 1910, the I.C.C. was further strengthened in the Mann-
Elkins Act. The systematic strengthening of this federal railroad
commission required that any state commissions with the same essential functions fall in line behind its leadership, an understanding that

was validated by the U.S. Supreme Court in both 1913 and 1914. As state commissions setting rates affecting interstate commerce thereafter operated according to the dictates of the I.C.C., the Southern Pacific transferred the focal point of its concerns from Sacramento to Washington, D.C. The Southern Pacific was not kicked out of California politics. It left voluntarily. Thereafter, getting the right people selected to the I.C.C. was the Southern Pacific's highest political priority, as it was for other railroad corporations.

Despite their exaggerated boasts regarding the Southern Pacific, the California progressives did inaugurate other significant reforms. Statewide, both women's suffrage and direct democracy (in the form of initiative, referendum and recall mechanisms), were in place by 1911. Early in the century, women's clubs throughout the state had taken the lead in calling for numerous reforms. Recognizing the key role that women had played in mounting the Progressive movement, California became the sixth state in the Union to allow women's suffrage. Almost another decade went by before the U.S. Constitution itself was amended to allow women nationwide to vote. Newly empowered, California's middle-class club women vowed to bring a new, higher moral tone to California life, as shown in 1913 by the state's criminalization of prostitution.

Seeds of the future welfare state were planted during the Progressive Era. State workmen's compensation for accidents on the job (agricultural occupations excluded) was initiated in 1913. Nonpartisanship, the idea that many modern governmental functions were beyond the appropriate sphere of traditional partisan politics, was also instituted at that time. As government acquired more administrative tasks in an urbanizing industrial environment, questions of efficient management became more important than any partisan considerations. Consequently, first on the local level and subsequently statewide, many elected governmental posts were designated "nonpartisan," as candidates' political affiliations were deemed irrelevant.

Unfortunately, there was a dark side to California progressivism that most directly involved Japanese immigrants. In the 1880s, white Californians had congratulated themselves on ending Chinese immigration to the United States, but shortly after that, Japanese immigration began. It swelled to a torrent following the Russo-Japanese War of 1904-1905, when oppressive taxation to pay for Japan's victorious war drove many Japanese from their homeland. Some emigrated to Hawaii, by then an American possession. Others went to the mainland United States, especially California.

In 1906, San Francisco's school board shunned these new-comers by erecting separate public schools for Japanese children. This created an international incident. Japan, empowered by its recent victory over Russia, angrily responded to official San Francisco's racist insult. Struggling to hold on to the Philippines in the Far East, the United States was most vulnerable in a region where Japan had just proven its military prowess. Following the San Francisco school board decision, Japan bluntly reminded President Roosevelt of this fact.

President Theodore Roosevelt sent his "Great White Fleet" around the world, primarily to impress Japan with American naval power. Here the fleet is seen en-tering San Francisco Bay on May 6, 1908. (Courtesy, U.S. Naval Historical Cen-ter).

The American president reacted. First, he persuaded the San Francisco school board to rescind its earlier segregating order. Second, he sent the American navy on a tour to Japanese waters, as if to emphasize that America could not be bullied. And he wrung from the Japanese a promise to halt the exodus of Japanese laborers to America—something desired by Californians. In this last action, called the Gentlemen's Agreement, only males were restricted. Given the skewed sex-ratio of Japanese immigrants already on America's shores, women were not included in the immigration ban. Accordingly, single Japanese men in California wrote home for picture-brides. Those women whose photographs won approval were soon on their way. Marriage and babies followed shortly after their arrival on the west coast. This development, in turn, created a new crisis as white Californians worried about the growing families of Japanese immigrants, and the term "yellow peril" thereafter became commonplace when discussing California's future demography.

As California's progressives achieved power statewide, white paranoia over Japanese immigration came to a head. While liberal on many issues, California's progressives typically reflected the white supremist assumptions of their time and place. In 1913, they enacted the Webb Alien Land Law, which was designed to keep Japanese immigrants from acquiring ownership of California real estate. Californians also began to call for Congress to enact a ban on all Japanese immigration, male and female, something that ultimately was done in 1924. Here was another national insult to Japan, which fostered anti-American feeling among a proud people.

The repercussions of California's negative relations with the Japanese lay in the future. Likewise, the full consequences of California's progressive political reforms could only fully be appreciated after the passage of many years. In hindsight we can see that of all their reforms, direct democracy perhaps had the greatest historic impact. After California became the nation's most populous state in the 1960s, California initiatives (resembling plebiscites on leading issues of the day) increasingly have shaped the nation's agenda. As direct democracy continues to be mostly non-existent at the federal level, its operation in the largest state has become a significant vehicle for the voice of the people in modern times.

Yet direct democracy often operates differently than imagined by the progressives themselves. They believed that the initiative would neutralize the political influence wielded by concentrated wealth. They were wrong. It has merely altered the way in which that influence is applied. Up to that point in time, the U.S. Senate had been dubbed "The Millionaires' Club," because wealthy candidates appeared to have an unfair advantage in swaying the votes of state legislatures. In the 1880s, Leland Stanford and George Hearst (the silver king and father of William Randolph Hearst) both had been elected U.S. Senators by the California state legislature. In hopes of ending "The Millionaires' Club," the Seventeenth Amendment to the U.S. Constitution was enacted in 1913, providing for the direct election of U.S. Senators, the federal government's only application of the direct-democracy mania of the Progressive Era. Yet, under the new regime of the people directly electing U.S. Senators, the Senate has largely remained a "Millionaires' Club," as it takes vast sums of money to wage a successful senatorial campaign to influence mass opinion.

In modern times, the initiative process has also been manipulated by the influence of concentrated wealth. Typically, corporate finances shape the initiative process in several ways. First, money is required to pay for numerous petition signature gatherers needed to put a measure on the ballot. Then, advertising time on television, radio, newspapers and billboards must be purchased to influence the numbers needed to carry the election. Corporate money can also confuse the entire process by financing rival initiatives designed either to lessen the impact of a proposed reform or to barrage the electorate with a variety of alternatives featuring technical implications that are difficult to comprehend.

Contrasting the power of money in the traditional legislative process with that in the initiative process can be instructive. In the former, money can influence the outcome through lobbying efforts that can prune a bill so that its original intent is dramatically altered. Sometimes this process works for the public interest, sometimes not. In the initiative process, there is no opportunity to alter a proposal. The only options are to vote for or against it as originally drafted. As such, initiatives at times are clumsy instruments for bringing about meaningful improvements. On the other hand, sometimes this process is the only way to break through a phalanx of special interests that effectively control a legislative body at any historical moment. In short, while direct democracy has not driven the power of money from the political process, it has significantly altered its role. In the initiative process, economic power can only be used to persuade. In those instances when the electorate directly enacts foolish legislation, the courts are present to review the enactment in light of proscriptions in the U.S. Constitution, the nation's fundamental law. Over the years, more than one momentarily popular California initiative has been subsequently killed in the courts.

In California and throughout the nation, the Progressive Era lasted until foreign affairs distracted the electorate in the maelstrom of World War I, which began in Europe in 1914 and drew the United States into its vortex in 1917. With that event, domestic reform largely ceased until the New Deal of the 1930s. When that later time arrived, changes in public policy began where the progressives had finished their work. On balance, the significant changes wrought by the progressives were few, but they provided the first thorough-going investigation and discussion of the many problems accompanying an urbanizing and industrializing society. As such, their reform movement was an appropriate entrée to the twentieth century.

Suggestions for Further Reading

1. Kevin Starr, *Inventing the Dream: California Through the Progressive Era* (1985).
2. William Deverell and Tom Sitton, eds, *California Progressivism Revisited and Revised* (1994).
3. Michael Kazin, *Barons of Labor: The San Francisco Building Trades and Union Power in the Progressive Era* (1987).
4. William B. Friedricks, *Henry E. Huntington and the Creation of Southern California* (1992).
5. Martin J. Schiesl, "Progressive Reform in Los Angeles Under Mayor Alexander, 1909-1913," *California Historical Quarterly*, 54 (Spring 1975), 37-56.
6. Tom Sitton, *John Randolph Haynes: California Progressive* (1992).
7. Mansel G. Blackford, *The Lost Dream: Businessmen and City Planning on the Pacific Coast, 1890-1920* (1992).
8. David D. Schmidt, *Citizen Lawmakers: The Ballot Initiative Referendum* (1989).
9. John M. Allswang, "The Origins of Direct Democracy in Los Angeles and California: The Development of an Issue and Its Relationship to Progressivism," *Southern California Quarterly*, 78 (Summer 1996), 175- 98.
10. Yuji Ichioka, *The Issei, The World of the First Generation Japanese Immigrants, 1885-1924* (1988).
11. Mitziko Sawada, "Culprits and Gentlemen: Meiji Japan's Restriction of Emigrants to the United States, 1891-1909," *Pacific Historical Review*, 60 (August 1991), 339-60.
12. Jacqueline R. Braitman, "A California Stateswoman, The Public Career of Katherine Philips Edson," *California History*, 65 (June 1986), 82-95.
13. Joan M. Jensen and Gloria Ricci Lathrop, *California Women, A History* (1987).

XII
WITHOUT BOUNDARIES: A DECADE OF
GLOBAL STRIFE, 1910-1920

Between 1910 and 1920, Californians increasingly realized the interdependent quality of local, national and international events destined to characterize the state's history in the twentieth century. Most did not like this dissolving of California's traditional boundaries. In the previous decade, Frank Norris' *The Octopus* had provided a window on this new condition. While the novel had been principally about Californians in a provincial setting, its author also provided his readers with a broader perspective of California wheat farms operating in a global economy that was beyond the ability of anyone to control.

The Octopus had inspired California's progressives, but not in its global aspects. Hiram Johnson had exploited the novel's most superficial portrayal of the Southern Pacific as a local demonic corporate force. The broader perspective of Norris' novel was lost on him. To a limited degree, Californians of the early twentieth century did have a global worldview of sorts, but it was an internationalism inspired by the likes of Josiah Strong. Strong had advocated a remodeled Manifest Destiny that projected the United States out upon the Pacific Rim, adding domains to an expanding American empire. The Spanish-American War of 1898 had advanced this crusade, and the opening of the Panama Canal in 1915 celebrated it further. In grand expositions, San Francisco and San Diego both anticipated a new California and new United States expecting to grow in world power following the rechanneling of maritime traffic through the locks spanning the Isthmus of Panama. Theodore Roosevelt's bullying manner in acquiring control of this new waterway for the United States fully characterized the American internationalism of Josiah Strong.

Hiram Johnson was willing to reap the economic benefits of this type of global perspective, but his heart was not oriented toward international concerns. His dreams were almost wholly domestic. He wanted to reform America, not get sidetracked into foreign affairs. Typical of progressives, he wanted to restore the virtues and ideals of America's lost rural past in a new urban setting. Thomas Jefferson's model of the independent yeoman farmer had long captivated the liberal sensibilities of Americans. Jefferson had worked to create an America in which equality of opportunity for the common person might be fully realized. This was the progressive's dream as well. Yet theirs was an urbanizing, industrial society, not an agricultural one as Jefferson had known.

In 1909, Herbert Croly's *The Promise of American Life* offered a philosophy for applying Jefferson's dream to the new industrial landscape. Croly's message was simple: Only by employing the nationalizing constitutional theories of Jefferson's mortal enemy, Alexander Hamilton, could Jeffersonian ends be realized in the twentieth century. Progressives were then centralizing governmental decision-making to restore equality of opportunity. President Theodore Roosevelt revealed this in his legislative program to bring back the "promise of American life." State-based reformers such as Hiram Johnson were willing to acquiesce in this new nationalist understanding. Specifically, the California reformer relied on Roosevelt's strengthened Interstate Commerce Commission to regulate the Southern Pacific, even as he claimed that his own state reforms had kicked the "Octopus" out of California politics.

Progressivism held together as a reform movement as long as this national domestic focus was maintained. Progressivism was willing to stretch traditional American provincialism beyond the boundaries of Jeffersonian states rights. Indeed, it encouraged a Hamiltonian national perspective. But when the nation's boundaries were reached, and the broader perspectives encouraged by World War I shattered their domestic blinders, progressives began to quarrel among themselves as to which course to take. Some, such as Woodrow Wilson, wanted to work toward a brave new world order. Others retained the dream that America could somehow remain apart from the Eastern Hemisphere, even as it invaded it as part of its own new economic Manifest Destiny. Hiram Johnson belonged to this latter school of thought.

Johnson had grown up in Sacramento, where his father Grove had served as a Southern Pacific political operative. Breaking with his father, Johnson had gone to San Francisco where he joined the progressive team prosecuting Boss Abraham Ruef. When Francis Heney, the lead prosecutor, was shot in open court by a prospective juror, Johnson took over the case. The notoriety resulting from his sending Ruef to prison propelled him directly into both statewide progressive politics and his election as governor in 1910. Over the next two years, Johnson orchestrated his legislature in a mad flurry of domestic reforms that captured the national imagination. By the time of the Republican nominating convention of 1912, he looked like a prospective candidate for high national office.

Johnson's opportunity lay in the Republican national convention in 1912, the most disruptive conclave in that party's long history. Theodore Roosevelt, who had left the presidency in 1909, attempted to bump his one-time friend and successor (President William Howard Taft) and seize the nomination for himself, ostensibly because Taft had gone soft as a reformer. The convention divided into pro-Roosevelt and pro-Taft factions, the latter controlling the Republican party apparatus as the Roosevelt forces stormed out to create the Progressive (Bull Moose) Party. Roosevelt was the obvious choice as the new Progressive Party's nominee for the presidency. And Hiram Johnson was chosen as Roosevelt's vice-presidential running mate.

Johnson's nomination for Vice President affected California politics for the next half century, if not longer. Thereafter, Republicans in California split into progressive and conservative factions. After bolting his party in 1912, Johnson was branded as a traitor by those who remained loyal to President Taft. The election of Democrat Woodrow Wilson in 1912, due solely to the split in the Republican Party, largely accounted for this animus. Johnson's standing in the Republican party was tarnished by this outcome. Additionally, the continuing presence of old Southern Pacific politicos in the state's Republican party leadership also fed an anti-Johnson attitude.

With so much hostility within his own party, Johnson could no longer be assured of success in future Republican party primaries. Accordingly, in 1913, he succeeded in getting his progressive legislature to enact a "cross-filing" law, allowing any candidate to run in as many party primaries as desired. So far as Johnson himself was concerned, cross-filing enabled him to run simultaneously in both the Republican and Progressive parties' primaries. Winning either one or both allowed him to be a candidate for reelection as governor in 1914.

For the next 50 years, cross-filing weakened party boundaries in California. With the demise of the Progressive party a few years after Johnson's reelection in 1914, Republican candidates often ran in both Republican and Democratic party primaries. In 1946, Republican governor Earl Warren won both major party primaries, blurring his own party affiliation in the minds of voters during an era when the Republican party was not popular. In 1959, a Democratic legislature finally succeeded in destroying this mechanism that had largely served to confuse party boundaries and make California politics focused more around personalities than party programs.

Ironically, just as Hiram Johnson installed cross-filing to strengthen his own cult of personality, California politics were becoming more influenced by ideological factors than ever before. Increasingly, local signs of a class struggle that seemed to be engulfing all of western civilization were evident. To a large degree the progressives themselves had been motivated by violent strikes in the 1890s to attempt to restore a classless society akin to their romanticized perception of America's rural past. Middle-class Americans had been drawn to the progressive crusade by this purpose. But as class warfare seemed to mount in state, nation and world in the second decade of the new century, the progressive dream increasingly appeared naive. As radical rhetoric became more strident and conservative resistance stiffened, progressives frequently were forced to choose sides in a struggle that they had failed to defuse. As governor of the state, Hiram Johnson was often at the center of this drama.

In 1910, a bomb destroyed the *Los Angeles Times* building, killing a score of victims. A subsequent trial revealed that this was the work of labor radicals from San Francisco, angered over the *Times'* policy of opposing unionization. That same year, radicals from the Industrial Workers of the World (I.W.W.) invaded Fresno, intent on raising class-consciousness throughout the San Joaquin Valley. This most radical of American unions was opposed to the conservative style of unionism represented by the American Federation of Labor (A.F.L.). The A.F.L. sought only to improve wages and job conditions. The I.W.W.'s goal was well beyond these boundaries and included a worker takeover of the means of production throughout the world. Any strikes or job actions they conducted were not primarily designed to win small victories in particular localities. Their goal was to change the consciousness of working people so that the latter could clearly identify their class enemies—all in preparation for a later revolution.

One common I.W.W. tactic was to descend upon a particular town. Arriving in Fresno in 1910 from all over the West, they began to preach on street corners against the police minions of their class oppressors. Arrested for disturbing the peace, they then stood four-square for American freedom of speech, violating any and all local ordinances designed to silence them. Their arrests clogged Fresno's

jail cells. Once behind bars, their incessant singing predictably led
their guards to brutal responses, such as turning fire hoses upon them
in their holding tanks to break their spirits. The bad publicity resulting from these repressive acts ultimately broke Fresno's resistance,
and the city fathers backed down in 1911, allowing the I.W.W. to
declare victory and leave town.

From Fresno, the I.W.W. next went to San Diego, where
they pursued the same tactics. Today, these events lack the emotional
content that they carried at the time. Many California progressives,
while ostensibly burning with a passion to restore a dying equality of
opportunity in a post-frontier America, were enraged by the "bums"
that they saw both in Fresno's and San Diego's so-called "Free Speech
Movements." Fresno's Chester Rowell, a leading progressive and
close friend of Hiram Johnson, made no secret of his contempt for the
Wobblies (I.W.W. members), as he whipped up community opposition against them in his *Fresno Republican.* "Which side are you on?"
is the lyric of a labor song, written decades later during the Great Depression. Increasingly, progressives were being forced to choose
which side they supported.

In 1913, violence erupted on Richard Durst's ranch in
Wheatland, in Yuba county. Durst's regular practice was to advertise
for more hands than he really needed, which allowed him to hire only
the most desperate workers for the lowest possible wages. The scene
was ideal for the I.W.W. No other union cared about the fate of California's migratory farm workers, many of whom were non-European
in origin and none of whom voted, due to their nomadic life style.
They were revolutionary tinder for anyone caring to light a spark to
their class consciousness.

"Blackie" Ford, an I.W.W. organizer, personally confronted
Durst and publicly challenged him regarding his blatant exploitation
of the working class. Thereupon, Durst called in the local sheriff, who
arrived with several deputies and other interested officials. One de-
puty sheriff fired a shot in the air to disperse a crowd of angry workers. A riot ensued in which the sheriff, the district attorney, and two
workers were killed; many more were injured. Governor Johnson sent
in the National Guard to restore order and then created a Commission
on Immigration and Housing to look into the conditions of migratory
farm workers. Its report revealed deplorable conditions. Nevertheless,
"Blackie" Ford and another I.W.W. agitator were tried for second-
degree murder and found guilty. They alone were blamed for the riot.

Progressives seemed immobilized by this outcome. In this struggle for class-consciousness, progressive spectators were being forced to take sides. Sympathetic governmental reports did not constitute adequate support in the eyes of radicalized workers. The process pained many like Johnson, who wanted to remain in a middle ground that was quickly eroding.

The next year, Charles T. Kelley organized a force of 1,500 unemployed farm workers to march on Sacramento, in much the same way that "Coxey's Army" had marched on Washington, D.C., twenty years before. The stated goal of "Kelley's Army" was to petition for state economic relief to accompany the progressives' acknowledgment of the deplorable working conditions of agricultural labor. Eight hundred deputized citizens drove the invading workers away from the capital. Radicals blasted Johnson for his handling of this and other confrontations. He in turn took notice of his critics, his hatred of them slowly coaxing him toward repression. While his public image was still very much that of a progressive reformer, internally he was beginning to move toward the reactionary positions that would come to characterize him in later life. Within himself, the boundaries between progressivism and a narrow conservativism were blurring.

In 1916, Thomas J. Mooney, one of Johnson's radical critics, was arrested for plotting and executing a murderous bomb-blast along the right of way of a parade in San Francisco, which had been designed to stir popular backing for America's entry into World War I. Radicals opposed the war as a capitalist struggle for imperialistic advantage and urged working people not to become unresisting cannon-fodder for their class enemies. Mooney, known for advocating the use of dynamite in "direct action," became a prime suspect in the San Francisco "Preparedness Day" Bombing. However, his subsequent conviction was seriously tainted. The chief witness against him was later proven to have lied under oath. Nevertheless, a widespread hatred of Mooney, shared by Hiram Johnson, kept him locked in San Quentin until 1939, when he was finally pardoned by a governor willing to risk offending public opinion.

Mounting radical activity contributed to Johnson's decision to run for the U.S. Senate in 1916. The middle ground needed for any effective progressive movement within California was rapidly disappearing. Under these conditions, leaving the state had definite attractions. Increasingly, he was receiving attacks from the left. And he continued to be attacked from the right. He was still detested by the

California Republican Party's conservative wing, who controlled his party's machinery. Indeed, in 1916, conservatives put up a rival candidate for the Senate to run against him in the Republican primary.

That year also included a presidential election. The national Republican convention picked New York progressive Charles Evans Hughes to run against President Wilson. Hughes had served as New York's governor until 1910, when President Taft had appointed him to the U.S. Supreme Court. His subsequent service on the bench had allowed him to avoid the messy struggle within the Republican party between progressives and conservatives in 1912. Accordingly, he was the ideal candidate in 1916 for a party wanting to heal its internal divisions.

Johnson was supportive of Hughes. They were both progressive Republicans. But the conservative Republicans who managed the Hughes campaign in California deliberately worked to keep Johnson and Hughes apart. Accordingly, the Hughes' campaign intentionally snubbed Johnson, who unsuccessfully sought an audience with Hughes during the latter's brief campaign swing through California. "The men surrounding Mr. Hughes in California and in charge of his tour," Johnson wrote at the time, "are much more interested in my defeat than in Mr. Hughes' election."

Hughes was used by his California handlers for a provincial vendetta that ultimately cost their candidate the presidency. Whereas Johnson went on to be elected to the senate by over 300,000 votes, Hughes lost to Wilson in California by 3,773 votes. On election night, with California one of the last states to report its returns, it appeared that Hughes had won. After all, California was then very much a Republican state. If Hughes had carried California, as had been expected, he would have been elected. When the results were finally known, many concluded that Hughes' botched campaign in California resulted in the reelection of Woodrow Wilson.

The consequences of this local event were far reaching. Wilson's second term witnessed a significant turning point in world history. The United States entered World War I and ended a bloody military deadlock with fresh American troops. In drafting the peace that followed, Wilson played a leading role in creating a new international legislature, the League of Nations. However, he ran into problems in selling his global vision to the American people. Senator Hiram Johnson fought him more than any other American political leader. Johnson seemed to regard Wilson's new international proposal as a conspiracy to sell out the United States. Always a most provincial man, Johnson regarded the decade's events, involving world war, as foiling domestic reform. Emotionally, his own "irreconcilable" war against the League was waged as a desperate last stand to get America to refocus upon domestic issues.

JOHNSON: "GIVE US A SQUARE LOOK AT THAT CHILD!"

Hiram Johnson sought to destroy the League of Nations, which was indeed President Wilson's "baby." (Cartoon by Arthur Buel. Courtesy, *The Sacramento Bee*)

As for Wilson, his own campaign against Johnson for the heart and soul of America broke his body if not his spirit. At Pueblo, Colorado, the President suffered a massive stroke on a scheduled tour designed to convince the public to support his League. With the president paralyzed and bedridden, the country drifted leaderless for the next two years. With a damaged and increasingly stubborn president who refused to compromise, the most powerful nation on earth retreated into the isolationism advocated by Hiram Johnson. As a result, the United States never did join the League of Nations. Unfortunately, without American participation, the new international organization was not in a strong position to maintain world peace in the trying years that followed.

The Bolshevik Revolution in Russia in 1917 further contributed to the various trends covered in this chapter. Fear of the I.W.W. grew, as to many American citizens its members appeared to be homegrown Bolsheviks. Accordingly, California's legislature enacted the Criminal Syndicalist Law of 1919. This measure virtually outlawed membership in any organization (such as the I.W.W.) that advocated revolution. It outlawed any speech that local police might deem revolutionary in nature. At the end of the decade, amidst the ruins of progressivism, California's electorate finally definitely chose which side to take in the international class struggle.

A literal reading of the Constitution's First Amendment reveals that its guarantee of free speech only bars restrictive action by Congress. As frightened states such as California began to restrict freedom of speech, liberal constitutional theorists began to dream of someday stretching the First Amendment to apply to the states by means of far more ambiguous language in the Fourteenth Amendment, which states that "liberty" is protected against arbitrary state legislation. But official sanction of that constitutional reinterpretation lay well in the future. As for California in 1919, traditional freedom of speech became highly tenuous.

In the twentieth-century's second decade, the boundary lines of California history expanded to take in the entire globe. Events in Moscow helped motivate actions by a California legislature. Likewise, the presidential campaign of 1916 in California shaped world events. While we cannot know how Charles Evans Hughes might have performed as president, we do know that the second term of Woodrow Wilson negatively influenced the future course of world history. The subsequent rise of Adolf Hitler was encouraged by the failure of Wilson's second term. Only those who believe in historical inevitability can argue that a Hughes presidency could have made no substantial difference.

Hiram Johnson's foray into national politics negatively affected California politics for the next half century. Cross-filing, a political band-aid designed to get Johnson through temporary Republican intra-party bad feelings, encouraged a personality politics that blurred any focus upon real issues. As for Johnson's senatorial career, his leap into national and international issues revealed him often at his worst. In the 1920s, he led the successful effort to ban all Japanese immigration to the United States. In the 1930s, he supported Charles Lindbergh's America First Committee to keep America upon an isolationist course as Hitler increasingly revealed his plans of world conquest. In the 1940s, he whined about British Prime Minister Winston Churchill determining the course of American foreign policy and refused to support the new United Nations, the successor of the League that he had earlier mortally wounded. Ironically, Johnson died on August 6, 1945, the day that the first Atom Bomb dropped in wartime exploded over Hiroshima. Despite his twenty-eight-year tenure in the Senate, he had failed to keep the United States and his native California in a condition of blessed isolation. Had he lived to appreciate the full impact of the chilling event of his death day, even he might have realized that increasingly California was without meaningful boundaries.

Suggestions for Further Reading

1. Richard C. Lower, *A Bloc of One: The Political Career of Hiram Johnson* (1993).

2. Irving McKee, "The Background and Early Career of Hiram Warren Johnson, 1866-1910," *Pacific Historical Review*, 19 (Feb. 1950), 17-30.

3. Spencer C. Olin, Jr., *California's Prodigal Sons: Hiram Johnson and the Progressives, 1911-1917* (1968).

4. James C. Findley, "Cross-Filing in California Politics," *Western Political Quarterly*, 22 (Sept. 1959), 699-711.

5. Ronald Genini, "Industrial Workers of the World and Their Fresno Speech Fight, 1910-1911," *California Historical Quarterly*, 53 (Summer 1974), 100-14.

6. Grace L. Miller, "The I.W.W. Free Speech Fight: San Diego, 1912," *Southern California Quarterly*, 54 (Fall 1972), 211-38.

7. A. Lincoln, "Theodore Roosevelt, Hiram Johnson, and the Vice-Presidential Nomination of 1912," *Pacific Historical Review*, 28 (Aug. 1959), 267-84.

8. Frederick M. Davenport, "Did Hughes Snub Johnson?" *American Political Science Review*, 43 (April 1949), 321-32.

9. Thomas G. Paterson, "California Progressives and Foreign Policy," *California Historical Society Quarterly*, 47 (Dec.1968), 329-42.

10. Cletus E. Daniel, *Bitter Harvest: A History of California Farmworkers, 1870-1941* (1981).

11. Carey McWilliams, *Factories in the Field* (1939).

12. Richard H. Frost, *The Mooney Case* (1968).

13. Howard A. DeWitt, "Hiram W. Johnson and World War I: A Progressive in Transition," *Southern California Quarterly*, 56 (Fall 1974), 295-305.

14. Woodrow C. Whitten, *Criminal Syndicalism and the Law in California, 1919-1927* (1969).

XIII
THE SUPREMACY OF LOS ANGELES AND ITS CHALLENGERS

In the 1920s, Los Angeles became California's leading city. Its rise had been steady following Los Angeles' nadir in the floods and droughts of the 1860s. First, it gained transcontinental rail facilities in the 1870s and came to enjoy competing transcontinental rail rates in the 1880s. In the following decade, Angelenos made the necessary steps to acquire a world-class man-made harbor that in the next century came to outdistance the fabled natural port of San Francisco for global traffic. One more major step was needed to insure Los Angeles' greatness, and that was the acquisition of outside water supplies in 1913, with the completion of the Los Angeles Aqueduct to the Owens River Valley on the eastern slope of the Sierra Nevada Mountains. Without this additional water, Los Angeles' growth would have been limited to approximately 250,000 people.

Rich oil discoveries in the 1890s, both in Los Angeles and in nearby Ventura County, made the region a leading petroleum production area nationwide. With the conversion of railroad locomotives from coal to oil and the concurrent rise of the automobile industry, petroleum became the key ingredient in the next wave of the industrial revolution. In the decade of the twenties, California became the premier oil producing state in the nation. With a rising automobile industry placing an increasing demand on petroleum products, Los Angeles enjoyed being at the center of a global economic transformation.

Unlike San Francisco, which prided itself on being a "closed shop" town, Los Angeles' businesses were largely free from the economic strictures imposed by labor unions. Harrison Gray Otis, publisher of the *Los Angeles Times*, ruthlessly fought unionization. Organized labor fought back, destroying the *Times* building with dynamite in 1910, with considerable loss of life. In a subsequent trial, the two principal defendants confessed in open court and thereby revealed an ugly underside to the labor movement. A public backlash from the *Times* bombing kept unionization weak in Los Angeles. The state's Criminal Syndicalist Law of 1919 further contributed to keeping Los Angeles "open shop," as it was used to break an I.W.W. strike at the booming port of San Pedro in 1923. Given a choice be-

tween San Francisco or Los Angeles, new business enterprise gravitated southward in part because of the latter's relatively weak unions.
Here was yet another cause of Los Angeles' overtaking of San Francisco as the queen city of the West.

Movies, a new medium in mass entertainment, took root in
the Los Angeles area early in the century. This too contributed to the
supremacy of Los Angeles. In the days before artificial lighting, good
weather was needed for shooting motion pictures. This factor, together with the geographic variety of deserts, mountains and ocean
scenes all existing within close proximity, made the greater Los Angeles area an inevitable center for American movie-making. For those
eastern film producers violating Thomas Alva Edison's patents on
movie-making machinery, Los Angeles' proximity to Mexico was
also most attractive. A quick trip across the border could frustrate
legal efforts to enforce Edison's legal rights. For a myriad of reasons,
Los Angeles (or rather nearby Hollywood) became America's movie
capital by World War I. The European war made Hollywood the
world's movie capital as well, as young European producers and actors were drawn into the maelstrom of the fighting engulfing their
homelands. Ironically, Charlie Chaplin, one of Hollywood's top stars
of the twenties, achieved his greatness only because he avoided military service to his native England.

Broadcasting images of American life throughout the nation
and the world, "Hollywood" and all of Los Angeles became a new
center of popular culture. Early on, the impact of this medium was
somewhat controversial. Many early films titillated audiences with
scenes of lightly veiled nudity. This, together with some early scandals involving the sordid private lives of actors and actresses, led the
motion picture producers themselves to engage in self-censorship in
hopes of avoiding a less desirable state censorship. Similar to the restrictions of the Criminal Syndicalist Law, state censorship of movies,
books or any other cultural material was then perfectly legal if a majority of the voters of a locality or state wanted it. In 1922, Hollywood moved to foreclose this possibility with the creation of a self-
censoring agency under the direction of Will Hays.

For the next generation, Hollywood produced films resting
solely upon the strength of their plots, the acting abilities of their
casts and the skills of their directors. With sexuality and violence
restrained in their themes, Hollywood entered upon its period of
world dominance. Later, after World War II, the Hays office crum-

bled amidst a competition of foreign films exciting emotions long forbidden in American movies. By that time, the nation's highest court began to apply the Bill of Rights to the states. Ultimately, these economic and constitutional changes encouraged American filmmakers eager to portray the darker side of human nature. But in the 1920s, Hollywood moved in the other direction.

In the 1920s, tourists were drawn to southern California by the glitter of Hollywood and the fabled weather of sunshine and surf that had inspired the earlier "Health Rush." The sweet fruits of citrus agriculture, growing in seemingly endless orchards throughout the greater Los Angeles basin, added to the region's charm that even the dirty derricks and the ever-present smell of crude oil in the more immediate vicinity of Los Angeles could not obliterate. And even the derricks added to the feeling of prosperity that affected all who visited the region, causing many to stay in hopes of achieving a better life.

As Los Angeles grew in numbers, San Franciscans mounted the political barricades. Under California's constitution, reapportionment was supposed to give more political power to growing regions. The Census of 1920 reported that San Francisco had lost its premier status and by rights and numbers that honor belonged to Los Angeles. Nevertheless, assemblymen and senators from San Francisco in the state legislature combined with those from rural districts to deny Los Angeles the additional representatives to reflect the change. Other states were going through similar processes as the rapid urbanization of the entire nation became fully apparent in the twenties. In many states, rural areas hung on desperately to their traditional control over state legislatures in an effort to keep new, upstart cities in their political place. In many such situations, there was nothing that the cities could do about remedying their plight. But in California the direct-democracy reforms of the progressives did provide a way to work fundamental change within the system despite the legislature's inaction. In 1926, Angelenos put an initiative on the ballot to force reapportionment.

San Franciscans could not bear to surrender to Los Angeles. For them, San Francisco was "the city" and Los Angeles some overnight creation reeking of a strange mixture of Midwestern provincialism and Hollywood garishness. San Francisco was cosmopolitan, having somewhat the air of a European city. Its denizens appreciated the opera. The Great Caruso himself had been in the city on the day of the great San Francisco earthquake of 1906. The Panama-Pacific International Exposition of 1915 had celebrated the city's reconstruction from that disaster. Over nineteen million people had visited this fair, which celebrated San Francisco's continuing dominance along the Pacific slope. Then, five years later, this was lost as the census revealed that Los Angeles had become California's largest city.

San Franciscans prided themselves on their sophistication. By contrast, Los Angeles seemed to represent small-minded folk who took the state's Criminal Syndicalist Act seriously and viewed labor unions as a foreign plot against Americanism. Upton Sinclair, the renown author of the progressive novel *The Jungle* (1906), was arrested for reading the Bill of Rights at a meeting supporting the strikers at San Pedro in 1923. "What city worthy of the name promoted such narrow-mindedness?" Liberal San Franciscans smugly asked themselves. Authorities in Los Angeles claimed that the socialist Sinclair had violated the Criminal Syndicalist Law; in San Francisco, the district attorney let it be known that this reactionary law would not be enforced in his city.

San Franciscans looked upon the modified Pentecostal religion of Los Angeles' Aimee Semple McPherson with veiled scorn. Her unique missionary activity among rootless migrants from the Midwest was viewed from the north as bizarre, at the very least. Her friendship with Charlie Chaplin and other Hollywood notables influenced her theatrical worship services, in which she chased away men in devil costumes. Her carnival-like performances and her promotional stunts to raise funds to build her Angelus Temple and then maintain herself in personal luxury offended even some Angelenos, especially those used to more sedate, mainline religion. Then came her mysterious disappearance in 1926. Supposedly, she drowned while swimming at a Los Angeles beach, only to turn up a month later on a Mexican desert, dressed in high heels and claiming that she had escaped from kidnappers. All the while rumors circulated that she had been with one of her male church employees in a Carmel love nest. Only such goings on could occur in tasteless Los Angeles, or so thought San Franciscans. San Franciscans did not necessarily mind Mrs. McPherson's tryst in Carmel. After all, "the city" itself was renown for both its risqué past and present. What bothered them was the hypocrisy of it all, especially her blatant denials to her Bible-belt parishioners.

The contrast between San Francisco and Los Angeles could also be seen in their universities. The Bay Area boasted the state's two premier institutions of higher education—the University of California at Berkeley in the East Bay and Stanford University down the peninsula. Los Angeles had the University of Southern California, which the cultural elite from the north regarded as an athletic department in search of a college, and U.C.L.A., which San Franciscans then called "the Southern Branch."

In the 1920s, Los Angeles's academic reputation dramatically improved as U.S.C. multiplied its professional schools, turning out doctors and engineers to serve its growing service area. U.C.L.A. gradually shed its fledgling image and became a valid research institution in its own right. In 1919, the creation of nearby San Marino's Huntington Library, which became a world-class research institution under the directorship of Frederick Jackson Turner, further added luster to Los Angeles' rising intellectual status, as did Pasadena's California Institute of Technology, which began to attract the world's top scientists in the 1920s. But in the minds of San Franciscans, Los Angeles could never fully catch up.

So far as San Francisco was concerned, their city, "the city," was corporate headquarters. A.P. Giannini's remolding of his Bank of Italy into the Bank of America during the 1920s, together with his founding of Transamerica Corporation in 1928, seemed to indicate that San Francisco-based enterprises continued to lead the state's business activity. By contrast, Los Angeles' economic tycoons were nouveau-riche movie makers and the likes of Edward L. Doheny, who was mired in a national oil scandal that ultimately destroyed the reputation of Warren G. Harding's presidential administration. "Teapot Dome" and "Doheny" were synonymous with political corruption in the decade. San Franciscans knew that their business leaders were of a better sort.

San Franciscans could also feel self-righteous reviewing Los Angeles's rape of the Owens River Valley. Before and during the 1920s, the City of Los Angeles bought out the water rights of farmers near the aqueduct bringing Owens Valley water to the Los Angeles basin. The small town merchants serving the Owens Valley bitterly complained of the lost trade as farmers moved away and the valley floor, stripped of water, reverted to desert. Bombings of portions of the aqueduct began to interrupt the flow of water to the southern metropolis. Then the full economic weight of Los Angeles was brought to bear against the local bankers leading the Owens Valley water war; and the valley was forced to surrender and become a fiefdom of Los Angeles. Thereafter, it served its master with bait shops and cafes for Angeleno sport fishermen and campers. San Francisco's collective heart went out to the valley residents, brutalized by the monstrous urban octopus known as Los Angeles.

Meanwhile, San Francisco's own environmental record was not clean. In 1923, San Francisco finished damming the beautiful

Hetch Hetchy Valley, as it looked in 1916, before San Francisco converted it into a reservoir. (Courtesy, City and County of San Francisco, Public Utilities Commission).

Hetch Hetchy Valley, located in the high Sierras just north of Yosemite. The Hetch Hetchy reservoir serving the water needs of San Francisco did not displace any people as in the Owens River Valley affair. Hetch Hetchy had simply been a scenic wonder. Filling with water in the twenties, its ancient beauty was destroyed. Except for John Muir's allies, who fought the development of Hetch Hetchy, San Franciscans generally understood the need for this project, but they could never condone Los Angeles' behavior in the Owens River Valley.

In large and small matters, San Franciscans scorned Los Angeles. Accordingly, they could not support Proposition 20, an initiative on the ballot in 1926 to give Los Angeles increased representation in the state legislature to recognize demographic changes. Instead, they backed Proposition 28, a rival initiative to restructure
California's legislature. Up to this point, both houses of the legislature
had represented people. San Francisco's initiative proposed to have
the assembly continue to represent people, but have the Senate represent counties, the preponderance of which were in northern California. It was called the "federal plan," because of its resemblance to the
structure of the federal Congress. Under this proposal, both San Francisco and Los Angeles, as well as all other California urban centers,
would lose seats in the state senate. But San Franciscans liked it because it would prevent Los Angeles from controlling the entire state
government.

Under the "federal plan," southern California would dominate in the assembly and control the governor's office, while northern
California would control the senate. The checks and balances of the
new system appealed to a statewide majority, as Proposition 28
passed and Proposition 20 went down to defeat in 1926. Using the
initiative process, designed by the progressive reformers to allow the
people to express their majoritarian will directly, California created a
new system of state government insuring that the minority views of
northern Californians would not be smothered by a new southern
California majority.

Over the subsequent four decades, numerous efforts were
made to resubmit the question to the people. California's direct democracy provided ample opportunity to overturn the new "federal
plan." Yet, in 1928, 1948, 1960 and 1961, initiative efforts to restore
proportional representation to both houses of the state legislature
were defeated. Similarly, six separate constitutional amendments introduced in the legislature to bring about the same result also lost out.
The people had spoken. They did not want a government that could
allow southern California to control California's government without
guarantees of significant input from northern California. A majority
of Californians believed that they had created a system of democratic
government well suited to meet the needs of their geographically divided state.

Then, in 1964, the United States Supreme Court, the least
democratic branch of the federal government, ruled that both houses

of the legislature in every state had to be based upon proportional representation. Ironically, this so-called "one man, one vote" decision was trumpeted as a victory for democracy. But it directly violated the democratic wishes of the majority of the people of California. Interestingly, a former governor of California (Chief Justice Earl Warren) wrote the opinion, even though as governor he had consistently supported the "federal plan" for California. The decision was based on an unprecedented judicial use of the "equal protection" clause of the Fourteenth Amendment, a usage never intended by the framers of that amendment. Of all of the instances of judicial activism during the years of the Warren Court, this decision (*Reynolds v. Sims*) stands out as the premier example. Warren himself regarded it as his most significant case. The fact that California quietly changed its form of government in 1965 (under court order) back to the way that it had looked before 1926, showed that ultimately the public did not feel very strongly about the exact nature of their statewide representation.

Critics of the "federal plan" noted that that system had given undue opportunities for political corruption as lobbyists had easily controlled senators elected from lightly populated rural counties. Indeed, small amounts of money had enabled notorious lobbyist Artie Samish to control rural senators in the late 1940s, and through them to direct the state senate. Nevertheless, a return to proportional representation has not cleansed the state legislature of corruption, as the legislative history of the state since 1965 has shown.

For California, the true significance of the court decision in 1964 is that it insured that thereafter southern California could control the government of California without any significant check from northern California. In the future, this fact is likely to be most ominous regarding the allocation of state water resources in periods of extended drought. As southern California is largely an arid region compared with the wetter north, the former might simply take what it needs from the latter under extreme conditions. Unless northern California some day splits away and becomes a separate state, there is no guarantee that this scenario will not one day occur.

Southern California's voracious thirst for more water has been evident since the twenties, if not before. By the mid-twenties, Los Angeles city planners could see that urban growth was outstripping Owens River water supplies. Without any outside water resources, San Diego was equally desperate. Southern California did not then control the state government, but it could and did exercise its political power in successfully appealing for federal assistance. At issue was the development and use of Colorado River water resources. Under a congressional bill co-authored by a San Bernardino congressman and Senator Hiram Johnson in 1928, a federal program commenced to construct a series of dams on the Colorado and apportion water to Los Angeles, San Diego and the Imperial Valley, the latter located due east of San Diego. While water from this new source would not be available for over a decade, the future growth of southern California was assured by the act.

In the 1920s, southern California proclaimed its newly won supremacy. It had been earned by astute decisions of earlier urban planners who had seen the need for railroad facilities and port development, as well as sufficient water resources to guarantee growth. Los Angeles' economic development attached itself to growth industries of the future—petroleum and motion pictures. Sunshine attracted visitors, arriving in the decade's favorite mode of transportation, the automobile. Many stayed, propelling further growth. Failing to achieve a political dominance to accompany its increasing economic might, southern California nonetheless continued to grow, reaching out to the Colorado River, a water basin beyond even California's ability to control.

Falling from preeminence in the twenties, San Franciscans held on at least to pretenses of cultural superiority. They bristled when outsiders, especially Angelenos, referred to their city as "Frisco." Athletic contests between regional champions such as Stanford and U.S.C. took on an aura of morality plays of Davidic virtue versus an amoral power of Goliath-like proportions. At least this attitude increasingly characterized the San Francisco Bay Area, sensitive to its diminishing status in comparison with the booming southern part of the state. As for Angelenos, they continued to love to visit quaint San Francisco. They felt little compulsion to persuade northern Californians of their region's supremacy, for it was just a fact that could not be denied.

Suggestions for Further Reading

1. Kevin Starr, *Material Dreams, Southern California Through the 1920s* (1990).

2. Robert M. Fogelson, *The Fragmented Metropolis: Los Angeles, 1850-1930* (1993).

3. Norman M. Klein and Martin J. Schiesl, eds., *Twentieth Century Los Angeles: Power, Promotion and Social Conflict* (1990).

4. Andrew Rolle, *Los Angeles: From Pueblo to City of the Future* (1981).

5. Ashleigh E. Brilliant, *The Great Car Craze: How Southern California Collided with the Automobile in the 1920s* (1989).

6. Edith Blumhofer, *Aimee Semple McPherson: Everybody's Sister* (1994).

7. William Issel and Robert W. Cherney, *San Francisco, 1865-1932: Politics, Power, and Urban Development* (1986).

8. Roger W. Lotchin, "The Darwinian City: The Politics of Urbanization in San Francisco Between the World Wars," *Pacific Historical Review*, 48 (Aug. 1979), 357-82.

9. Felice A. Bonadio, *A. P. Giannini: Banker of America* (1994).

10. Gregg R. Hennessey, "San Diego, the U.S. Navy, and Urban Development: West Coast City Building, 1912-1929," *California History*, 72 (Summer 1993), 129-49.

11. Dan LaBotz, *Edward L. Doheny: Petroleum, Power and Politics in the United States and Mexico* (1991).

12. Gerald T. White, "California's Other Mineral," *Pacific Historical Review*, 39 (May 1970), 135-54.

13. Jules Tygiel, *The Great Los Angeles Swindle: Oil, Stocks, and Scandal During the Roaring Twenties* (1994).

14. Norris Hundley, Jr., The Great Thirst: Californians and Water, 1770-1990s (1992).

15. Abraham Hoffman, *Vision or Villain: Origins of the Owens Valley-Los Angeles Water Controversy* (1992/1981).

XIV
CAPITALISM'S FAILURE IN CALIFORNIA

The Great Depression of the 1930s terminated the ebullience of the twenties. Following the stock market crash of 1929, many concluded that capitalism had failed. Millions were suddenly unemployed. The presidential administration of Herbert Hoover searched for ways to alleviate the crisis. Federal agents in Los Angeles deported immigrants from Mexico who had come during the happier growth years of the city's recent past. Their labor was no longer needed as the once vibrant capitalist system stagnated. The fact that some American citizens were removed in this effort was generally ignored, due to both racism and the deepening of the economic crisis.

Back in the 1890s, historian Frederick Jackson Turner had suggested that the ending of the American frontier would inevitably produce a drying up of economic opportunity for the common person. The increasing severity of the depressions of the 1870s, the 1890s, and subsequently the 1930s seemed to prove his point conclusively. Franklin Roosevelt, the Democratic presidential candidate in 1932, latched onto this pessimistic theme throughout the campaign. In a speech before the Commonwealth Club in San Francisco, he most clearly articulated that the era of individualistic economic opportunity passed with the ending of the frontier. From that premise, he jumped to the conclusion that entrepreneurial creativity was likewise necessarily permanently discouraged. He lauded capitalism's productive power, but emphasized that the principal challenge facing America's future involved equitable distribution of the fruits of American industry. He held out little hope for increasing the nation's wealth. Instead, he assumed that capitalism had already reached its productive apex.

Roosevelt's solution was a "New Deal" for the American people that initially resembled planned scarcity more than shared abundance. Once elected and inaugurated, Roosevelt created new federal agencies designed to restrict both agricultural and industrial production in an effort to raise commodity prices. In agriculture, the Agricultural Adjustment Administration paid farmers not to produce. Crops already in the fields were destroyed. Baby pigs already born were slaughtered to keep from further glutting a market already "oversupplied" with pork products. In industry, the New Deal looked the same. Roosevelt's National Recovery Administration (NRA) developed industry-wide codes among participating companies to restrict industrial output. Firms cooperating with this effort were encouraged to display the NRA's blue eagle symbol to enlist public enthusiasm to save American capitalism by governmental restrictions.

Roosevelt's activity encouraged many. At the same time, he alienated various constituencies. He outraged a conservative minority by his governmental tinkering, but his sharpest critics were on the left. The latter saw him as not doing enough to meet the needs of desperate millions. Louisiana's Governor Huey Long lambasted the new president for offering the common person little more than the failed policies of his Republican predecessor. Governor Long demanded a program of income redistribution which called for a far greater socioeconomic leveling than that hoped for by Roosevelt, By contrast, all Roosevelt offered the common person was low-wage, make-work employment under several new federal agencies.

In the midst of this growing debate over how to deal politically with the collapse of capitalism, the California gubernatorial campaign of 1934 seized the national attention. Upton Sinclair, who broadcast his campaign to "End Poverty in California" (EPIC), became the Democratic party's nominee for governor. During the Progressive Era, Sinclair had won fame as a novelist exposing evils in the meatpacking industry. Subsequently, he moved to California and became an advocate for socialist causes. Throughout the twenties, he ran several times as the Socialist Party's candidate for governor. The Great Depression offered him new political opportunities, and he took advantage of California's direct primary law to win the state's Democratic primary. Democratic Party functionaries were chagrined that this Socialist had become their party's nominee for governor by going over their heads directly to a suffering people.

Sinclair's proposed program was the antithesis of Roosevelt's New Deal. Where Roosevelt used government to cut back on production, Sinclair called for using government to increase production. Sinclair belittled as heartless and cruel the traditional capitalist supply-and-demand economic theories that guided Roosevelt. Cutting back on production, he argued, made no sense when there were millions of people who were lacking the necessities of life. He promised voters that if he were elected, the state of California would take over both abandoned farms and factories and put them into productive use,

This cartoon by McWhorter, taken from the *EPIC News*, June 4, 1934, is clearly hostile to Franklin Roosevelt's program, referring to it as "Stale Bread and Old Clothes...." The drawing suggests that only by unlocking the factory gate with the EPIC Plan key will workers again experience prosperity. The EPIC symbol of a busy bee not so subtly criticized the New Deal's method of forcing worker inactivity in a capitalist attempt to raise prices for necessary commodities.

employing those without work to operate them. He envisioned a gigantic barter system of both collective farms producing foodstuffs needed for workers in the cities and state factories producing mer-

chandise needed by the state's farm workers. His dream was to erect a
socialist economy within California, the existence of which would
challenge Roosevelt to create something similar for the nation as a
whole.

Sinclair's campaign put Roosevelt in a quandary. The president could not afford to reject outright California's Democratic gubernatorial nominee. At the same time, he could not endorse Sinclair
without totally undermining the rationale of his own New Deal. And
so, in characteristic fashion, he met with Sinclair and engaged in
charming conversation that avoided any direct confrontation while at
the same time not officially endorsing him for governor of California.
Influential mainline Democrats in California accurately read Roosevelt's true political intent and refused to support Sinclair in the gubernatorial contest. The result was the election of Frank Merriam, a conservative Republican in the mold of Herbert Hoover, during the very
depths of the Great Depression.

Historians normally focus upon a vicious Republican media
campaign, conducted by Hollywood's Louis B. Mayer, as the chief
cause of Sinclair's defeat. Operating for the Merriam campaign,
Mayer made phony newsreels showing tramps and vagabonds de-
scending upon California in anticipation of Sinclair's victory. Likewise, he conducted filmed "interviews" in which Anglo-Americans
proudly announced their intentions to vote for Merriam, while Russian émigrés with thick beards and thicker accents proclaimed themselves for Sinclair. As Joseph Goebbels was designing his own
propaganda machine in Nazi Germany, Mayer was a cynical fron-
tiersman in the use of modern media in democratic campaigning.
Nevertheless, it is hard to believe that a mere media blitz was primarily responsible for Sinclair's defeat in the midst of a demoralizing
depression that directly and negatively affected the day-to-day life of
millions. Rather, the key fact is that most of those suffering economic
hardship had placed their faith in Franklin Roosevelt's leadership; and
many of them felt that they could not afford to undermine his program by voting for Sinclair.

Sinclair's defeat in 1934 and Huey Long's assassination in
1935 somewhat eased Roosevelt's political problems. Republican
Frank Merriam promised full cooperation in carrying out New Deal
programs in California. Nevertheless, many Californians continued to
dream of the possibilities of Sinclair's failed EPIC campaign. One of
these was novelist John Steinbeck, who wrote on themes of rural

poverty and human struggle, frequently set in his familiar home envi-
rons of Salinas and Monterey. In 1939, he published his greatest
work, *Grapes of Wrath*, a tale of impoverished dirt farmers migrating
to California from Dust-Bowl Oklahoma. This Pulitzer Prize winning
novel fully captured the Sinclair supporters' anger toward both the
failed capitalist system and Roosevelt's efforts to save it. Chapter
Twenty Five of the novel was directly aimed at Roosevelt's program
of cutting back on production at a time of extreme want. Steinbeck
wrote:

> Men with hoses squirt kerosene on the oranges....
> A million people hungry, needing the fruit--and
> kerosene sprayed over the golden mountains.
> And the smell of rot fills the country. Burn cof-
> fee for fuel in the ships. Burn corn to keep warm,
> it makes a hot fire. Dump potatoes in the rivers
> and place guards along the banks to keep the
> hungry people from fishing them out. Slaughter
> the pigs and bury them, and let the putrescence
> drip down into the earth. There is a crime here
> that goes beyond denunciation.

While having conservative Republican governors throughout
most of the Depression decade, California remained a hot-bed of
radical activity constantly challenging Roosevelt's New Deal to move
leftward. The depression was severe in the state, given its partial reliance on tourism and luxury items. During hard times, people spent
their resources only on absolute necessities, and so vacations to California were few. Citrus agriculture was especially hard hit. By bold
experimenting in new genre films, Hollywood successfully met the
common challenge facing all luxury products. New movies featured
murderous gangsters (played by new stars such as Edward G. Robinson, James Cagney, and Humphrey Bogart) and unearthly monsters of
various sorts (played by the likes of Bela Lugosi, Lon Chaney, Jr.,
and Boris Karloff). Other movies with triumphant, upbeat themes
offered a temporary escape from the real hardship waiting outside the
movie theaters' darkened halls. New technologies, such as color films
at the end of the decade, also kept impoverished fans interested and
willing to spend their precious coins. Having introduced talking films
in 1927, the motion picture industry managed to do well, even in

these bad times, But other "luxury" enterprises suffered, and many Californians bore the brunt of this. Their economic hard times generated radical thinking and sometimes action.

In San Francisco, a general strike during July 16-19, 1934, following a clash between longshoremen and police that resulted in loss of life ("Bloody Thursday," July 5), evidenced the muscle of union tradition in that city. More profoundly, the general strike raised the specter of class warfare. Harry Bridges, an immigrant from Australia who worked his way to the top of San Francisco's International Longshoreman's Association, led the strike and revealed the latent power of average working people over American capitalism. President Roosevelt had already been encouraging a strengthening of labor unions by the inclusion of Section 7a in the National Industrial Recovery Act, but he took notice of the working-class rage exhibited in the San Francisco general strike to push for the adoption of a far more comprehensive measure (the Wagner Act or National Labor Relations Act), which passed one year later. This legislation put the full weight of the federal government behind working people's right to organize unions and bargain collectively with their employers. More labor violence followed this, as employers were used to having the government on their side and had to learn through multiple strikes that the Wagner Act of 1935 had fundamentally changed management/labor relations.

Southern California also contributed to the leftward drift of the New Deal. In 1933, Dr. Francis E. Townsend, an unemployed physician from Long Beach, began a movement to pressure the federal government to provide pensions for every unemployed senior citizen in the country. His plan to revive the economy involved elderly people giving up their jobs to younger workers. In turn, the federal government was then to provide these old folks with generous pensions. In 1933, Townsend wrote, "We cannot kill off the surplus workers as we are doing with our hogs.... We must retire them from business activities and eliminate them from the field of competitive effort." According to Townsend, elderly people spending their entire monthly pension would further stimulate the economy, and the country would come out of the depression. His solution was seductive in democratic politics, and Roosevelt moved to incorporate some very modest federal assistance to seniors in the scope of his evolving New Deal. The result was the Social Security Act of 1935. At first, the amount provided each retiree was so small that it could not be considered a legitimate pension. But over the years the sum has grown, and many now regard Social Security pensions as a fundamental entitlement. The California-based Townsend Movement, as well as Sinclair's gubernatorial campaign, encouraged this significant reform.

After the enactment of the Social Security Act, Californians kept up the pressure for meaningful governmental pensions for retired people. Using the state's initiative process, the Ham 'n Eggs (or Thirty Dollars Every Thursday) plan was put on the ballot in 1938 and 1939. It was designed to get the state government to provide old age pensions of thirty dollars a week, paid in state scrip. Reputable economists and even Upton Sinclair came out against the proposal, given that it was unworkable as designed. The plan falsely assumed that in lieu of federal currency, shops and stores would accept state scrip for merchandise and groceries. Both in 1938 and in 1939 it was defeated, but its place on the ballot revealed that many Californians were angry and demanded more than what Roosevelt's New Deal was providing to meet their needs.

Meanwhile, Roosevelt's New Deal encouraged huge dam-building projects to generate employment opportunities. The construction of Boulder (Hoover) Dam and related lesser dams designed to control the Colorado River was the earliest of these. Los Angeles' and San Diego's potential water supplies especially benefited from this enterprise. In addition, the U.S. Bureau of Reclamation took over California's Central Valley Project in 1935, involving the construction of Friant Dam on the San Joaquin River. Many more rivers draining into the Sacramento and San Joaquin Valleys were dammed as well as part of this effort, which helped greatly expand irrigated agriculture in California's interior breadbasket, thereby insuring that the state would long remain the nation's premier agricultural producer. Migrants from the hard-stricken Dust-Bowl states of the Midwest sensed an opportunity and began their historic invasion of the San Joaquin Valley. Their arrival was not welcome among most Californians despite novelist John Steinbeck's best efforts to persuade them otherwise. Workers in the state opposed sharing scarce work opportunities with "outsiders," The decade had begun with Mexicans being expelled from the state in a federal deportation drive. It ended with a state-based effort to keep dispossessed Dust-Bowl victims out of California. The legislature's "Okie Law," which was enacted in the late thirties to bar indigents from entering the state, was quickly challenged in the courts. In 1941, the United States Supreme Court made its final determination in *Edwards v. California*. The court ruled that California had unconstitutionally attempted to interrupt interstate commerce, and the law was declared null and void. In the 1880s, California had succeeded in blocking Chinese immigration by getting the Congress to enact its prejudice. In the 1920s, they kept Japanese immigrants out as well by the same means. Early in the 1930s, Mexicans also were kept out with the aid of federal authorities. But with the "Okies," the federal government stymied provincial California's efforts to seal its borders against this latest perceived threat from the outside. The coming of world war and a resultant influx of newcomers from many quarters was soon to alter fundamentally California's traditional provincial world view.

California's Population of Mexican Origin or Descent, 1900-1960	
1900	8,086
1910	33,694
1920	88,771
1930	191,346
1940	134,312
1950	162,309
1960	695,643

California's population of Mexican origin or descent declined in 1930s due to federal deportations. (Data from David E. Lorey, ed., *United States-Mexico Border Statistics Since 1900, 1990 Update*, p. 112).

By the time that the last Ham 'n Eggs initiative appeared on the California ballot, war had already broken out in Europe. Within a year, France fell to Hitler's legions. Despite official neutrality, a shocked and frightened nation allowed President Roosevelt to place American industry on a wartime footing. In the late 1930s, European nations were increasingly shopping for the tools of war. American factories met this demand and the nation began to come out of the depression. With the fall of France, Great Britain stood alone against the Nazi war machine. Exercising bold leadership, Roosevelt engineered his Lend-Lease program through Congress, whereby America financed the defense of Britain (and subsequently the Soviet Union). With the coming of war, massive deficit spending to meet the international crisis brought the nation and California out of the Great Depression.

California received more than its proportional share of this war-related spending. One of the nation's aircraft industrial centers was already in southern California, and the federal monies financing resistance to Naziism only encouraged its further development. America's own subsequent entry into the war made California the leading beneficiary of what has come to be called "defense spending." The state became the nation's leading embarkation center for the Pacific Theater. In addition, aircraft production and ship building fed a tremendous economic boom. Unfortunately, this phenomenon turned into an entrenched economic way of life, as World War II eventually evolved into the Cold War, and more and more Californians become affected by federal dollars invested in the manufacture of war materiel.

Franklin Roosevelt had started his New Deal by federal manipulation of the supply and demand curves of traditional capitalist economics. This had evoked criticism from California's Upton Sinclair. The United States Supreme Court severely damaged Roosevelt's early New Deal by finding both the National Industrial Recovery Act and the Agricultural Adjustment Act unconstitutional. Roosevelt then moved leftward by enacting the Wagner Act and the Social Security Act, both in part inspired by events in California. But still the country remained in depression. Only the commencement of massive defense spending finally got the capitalist economy back on course.

Throughout the 1930s, many Californians, especially those who supported Upton Sinclair, believed that capitalism had failed and could never recover. If the state had entered into Sinclair's EPIC program, California indeed would have taken serious steps toward the construction of a socialist economy. Looking back to these events, we should consider their meaning for us today when many commonly assume that socialism has proven itself a failed system. Carrying the burden of a tremendous national debt that began as a cure for the Great Depression, has American capitalism truly moved beyond the flawed system that existed in the thirties? At the end of the century, many questions face the nation as it attempts to curb annual deficits: If meaningful measures are taken in our own time to balance systematically and consistently our annual governmental budgets, will the social fabric again be ripped apart as it was during the days of the Great Depression? Are a thoroughgoing socialism on the model advocated by Sinclair and a largely unrestricted free market capitalism of the kind that so disastrously failed in 1929 the only viable options?

Or is some hybrid mixing these two extremes (as eventually advocated by Franklin Roosevelt) the best system that can be contrived in an imperfect world? At the close of the century, Americans continue to wrestle with these questions.

Suggestions for Further Reading

1. Mark Reisler, "Always the Laborer, Never the Citizen: Anglo Perceptions of the Mexican Immigrant During the 1920s," *Pacific Historical Review*, 45 (May 1976), 231-54.

2. Douglas Monroy, "Like Swallows at the Old Mission; Mexicans and the Racial Politics of Growth in Los Angeles in the Interwar Period," *Western Historical Quarterly*, 14 (Oct. 1983), 435-58.

3. Francisco E. Balderrama and Raymond Rodriquez, *Decade Of Betrayal: Mexican Repatriation in the 1930s* (1995).

4. Camille Guerin-Gonzales, *Mexican Workers and American Dreams: Immigration, Repatriation, and California Farm Labor* (1994).

5. George Sanchez, *Becoming Mexican American: Ethnicity, Culture and Identity in Chicano Los Angeles, 1900-1945* (1993).

6. Martha Menchaca, *The Mexican Outsiders: A Community History of Marginalization and Discrimination in California* (1995).

7. William H. Mullins, *The Depression and the Urban West Coast, 1929-1933: Los Angeles, San Francisco, Seattle and Portland* (1991).

8. Kevin Starr, *Endangered Dreams: The Great Depression in California* (1995).

9. Richard Lowitt, *The New Deal and the West* (1984).

10. David Wellman, *The Union Makes Us Strong: Radical Unionism on the San Francisco Waterfront* (1995).

11. John Kagel, "The Day the City Stopped," *California History*, 63 (Summer 1984), 212-23.

12, Greg Mitchell, *The Campaign of the Century: Upton Sinclair's Race for Governor and the Birth of Media Politics* (1992).

13. Tom Zimmerman, "Ham and Eggs, Everybody!" *Southern California Quarterly*, 62 (Spring 1980), 77-96.

14. James N. Gregory, *American Exodus: The Dust Bowl Migration and Okie Culture in California* (1989).

15. George G. Rising, "An EPIC Campaign: Upton Sinclair's 1934 California Gubernatorial Campaign," *Southern California Quarterly*, 79 (Spring 1997), 101-24.

XV
CALIFORNIA'S WARFARE STATE

Historians debate the degree of change that World War II wrought for California. On one side are those that argue that many of the elements normally associated with that war—the rise of defense industries and a strong military presence in the state—were already observable before the war began. San Diego was a navy town long before the Japanese bombed Pearl Harbor. The turn of the century vision of the United States becoming a two-ocean naval power had already transformed San Diego by the time of World War I. In 1915, the Panama Canal was fully operational and the establishment of major army and navy bases in San Diego during World War I set the tone of that city well before the 1940s. Before World War II, the aircraft factories of Consolidated Vultee (Convair) and Ryan were also in San Diego. Southern California also boasted Lockheed, Douglas, North American and Northrop well before Pearl Harbor. Indeed, the Japanese surprise attack on Hawaii may have actually hindered southern California's growth toward complete domination in the rising aircraft industry by demonstrating just how vulnerable American holdings on the Pacific Rim were to Japanese naval and air power.

Nevertheless, World War II had a tremendous impact upon the development of the state. As mentioned in the last chapter, the war pushed California's economic development ever more toward a long-term dependency upon incoming federal "defense" dollars. During the war, San Diego, Los Angeles and San Francisco all became embarkation depots for the Pacific theater. Henry J. Kaiser, who early in the century began building highways and hydroelectric dams in the Far West, became the nation's largest shipbuilder during the war because of his multiple plants throughout the Bay Area and at San Pedro. His dam building activities in the 1930s had led him to construct the largest cement plant in the world before the war, which in turn generated his steel production operations at Fontana, located just west of San Bernardino. By examining the career of Kaiser and his industries one can readily observe the impact of the war on the economic history of the state.

The demand for labor in war-related industries radically changed California. Housewives went to work in both ship yards and aircraft plants. While the phenomenon of "Rosie the Riveter" lasted only during the war, a genera-

Women workers pose with their male supervisor under camouflage nets in August 1944 at the Douglas Aircraft plant in Long Beach.

tion later the lingering memory of their increased status during the war encouraged American women to renew the social experiment on a more permanent basis. In addition, the first large immigration of African Americans to the state occurred during World War II. Blacks had been present throughout California history. They had helped found Los Angeles in 1781. They had been in the California gold rush. But their overall numbers had been small in the state before World War II. The convergence of the invention of an automatic cotton-picking machine and the rise in war-related industrial employment opportunities in California encouraged black migration from the Southern states westward. Poor whites came out of the South as well. Labor-starved California which had shunned the "Okies" the decade before now welcomed all available hands.

An open invitation was extended to all but Japanese-Americans. Between the world wars, Japanese immigration to the United States had been barred, largely because of political pressure from California. Nevertheless, earlier Japanese immigrants and their offspring had prospered in California; and by the time of the Pearl Harbor attack, Japanese-American truck farmers dominated California's production of fresh fruits and vegetables. However, the war abruptly eliminated their presence in California agriculture. Viewed as potential enemies within, they were taken away from coastal areas and herded into scattered "relocation" centers run by federal authorities.

White California called out hysterically to intern all Japanese-Americans; and politicians, from President Roosevelt on down, readily responded. Not only were non-citizens arrested; even American citizens of Japanese ancestry were put into camps guarded by the United States Army. District by district, Japanese-Americans living in the Far Western states were forced to dispose of their property within a matter of days. Many sold all that they had for pennies on the dollar. Few today dispute that this massive violation of civil liberties is perhaps the ugliest episode of America's involvement in World War II.

That which happened to Americans of Japanese Ancestry (A.J.A.s) along the Pacific coast is often compared to events in Hawaii. In Hawaii, Japanese-Americans not immediately suspected of disloyal activity were not removed from their homes and neighborhoods. In Hawaii, A.J.A.s were employed in the war effort throughout the conflict. Yet the two situations being reviewed—that of Hawaii and California—were not comparable. A provision in the United States Constitution allows federal authorities to institute martial law when immediate danger threatens. Article I, Section 9, Paragraph 2, permits a termination of civil liberties "when in cases of rebellion or invasion the public safety may require it. Military authorities interpreted the Pearl Harbor attack of December 7, 1941, as an "invasion," and all civil liberties ended in Hawaii at the very beginning of the conflict. Freedom of speech and press ceased to exist. Normal rights, such as trial by jury, were suspended. Overnight, a military dictatorship was erected in Hawaii. Ironically, this fact alone prevented any "relocation" of Hawaii's Japanese-Americans.

Histories of the period regularly claim that the need for Japanese-American labor in Hawaii was the primary reason why Hawaii and California treated their Japanese-American citizens differently. This is not the case. Even after martial law was instituted in the islands, President Roosevelt himself wanted all of Hawaii's Japanese-Americans herded onto the island of Molokai and kept there for the duration of the war, irrespective of any labor considerations. He was informed by Hawaii's military authorities that that was unnecessary, as martial law kept the islands' Japanese-American residents firmly under federal control. Military police patrolled their neighborhoods. Their short-wave radios and cameras were confiscated. They were forbidden from fishing off shore, for fear that they might communicate with Japanese submarines. They were required to speak only in English on the telephone, where their conversations were monitored. Nothing like this was possible in California.

California was never attacked. Therefore, there was no possibility of ever triggering the Constitutional clause allowing the military to take over all of California government and society. In the early months of the war, one lone Japanese submarine did surface off of Goleta, just north of Santa Barbara. Several shells were lobbed at a small oil refinery there before the submarine left. This incident created a regional panic, especially in Los Angeles. But it hardly constituted an "invasion." The fact that California was a state in the Union, and not merely a federal territory as was Hawaii, was also significant. Probably something even greater than an airborne attack of the magnitude of Hawaii's December 7th experience would have been needed to close down California's state government. In any case, freedom of speech, freedom of the press and democratic government in general remained active in California throughout the war. Ironically, this fact principally accounts for the internment of Japanese Americans along the West Coast during World War II.

In California in the early months of the war, every democratic forum from city councils to the state legislature simply magnified the public's hysteria. California's free press equally served a negative role. Bigotry and prejudice were allowed free rein. The contrast with Hawaii is most instructive. In Hawaii, military authorities censored all newspapers before they went to press in an effort to keep the public calm. By reading the pages of both the *Honolulu Advertiser* and the *Los Angeles Times* in the early months of the war, one might conclude that Honolulu was in some hidden-away safe haven in the Midwest and Los Angeles was a vulnerable island immediately off the coast of Japan.

The public hysteria was understandable. At the outbreak of the war airborne radar had not yet been invented, and California's coastal communities could not be assured by authorities that the entire Japanese navy was not closing in for an attack. Democratic mores allowed that hysteria to develop unchecked along the West Coast, while in Hawaii all scare talk was silenced by the military. Interestingly, all of the rumors circulating in California about the duplicitous behavior of Japanese-Americans during the Pearl Harbor attack originated among Hawaii's whites, whose diatribes were published in California while being censored in Hawaii. As a result, Hawaii's Japanese-Americans fared much better than their relatives in California. Had Hawaii retained democracy during the early months of the war, something akin to "relocation" would certainly have happened there as well, irrespective of labor considerations.

Ironically, the United States Supreme Court later declared Hawaii's martial law unconstitutional, while upholding "relocation" along the West Coast which had much less potential constitutional backing. In *Duncan v. Kahanamoku* (1946), the Court ruled that any constitutional reason for martial law in Hawaii disappeared after the Japanese defeat at Midway in June 1942. Yet in a series of cases involving the constitutionality of "relocation" along the West Coast, the Court effectively ruled that a vague "military necessity" can void the Bill of Rights in wartime. After the war, this sorry legal history festered. Eventually, in 1988, Congress granted a "redress" of $20,000 in damages for each of those Japanese Americans put through the "relocation" experience.

The removal of Japanese Americans from California agriculture during the war created a labor problem of its own. In addition,
the war stripped additional workers from the farms as new, better
industrial job opportunities could be found in California's cities. Not
surprisingly, the federal government went to Mexico to solve extreme
wartime labor shortages in California agriculture. Having deported
Mexican workers from California during the Depression, the United
States now reversed course. In 1942, the Department of Agriculture
inaugurated the so-called "bracero program" to bring Mexican farm
workers into California. After the war was over, the program continued, due to the fact that domestic workers could not be found to do
such hard labor for the low wages that were traditional in California
agriculture.

John Steinbeck's *Grapes of Wrath* (1939) had presented the
plight of exploited California farm workers in the genre of fiction.
Carey McWilliams' *Factories in the Field* (1939) documented the
worst of Steinbeck's impressionistic findings. Growing food was big
business in California, which enjoyed the status as the premier
agricultural state in the nation. Both the scope of production and the
diversity of its farm products were rivaled by no other state. During
seasons when other states could not produce fresh fruits and
vegetables, California could deliver at prices that pleased consumers.
All of this was due not only to excellent climate, good soil and
publicly financed irrigation projects but also a ready supply of
inexpensive labor. The bracero program insured that the latter could
last almost indefinitely.

Given the extreme poverty of Mexican farm workers, California's southern neighbor could be counted upon to supply cheap
labor. Some came through the government-sponsored bracero program. Others simply crossed over the border on their own looking for
work. The result was that Mexicans became familiar with the state.
Many stayed, creating a long-term trend that gradually reshaped the
demographic profile of California. In 1964, under pressure from
emerging farm workers unions to improve the lot of domestic migratory farm labor, the bracero program came to an end. But a growing
Latino presence in the state remained. This trend had actually begun
early in the century, but the deportation drives of the 1930s had temporarily stalled it. California's need for Mexican labor during the war
reactivated the trend, which has remained in place ever since.

The presence of growing numbers of African Americans and Latinos in California led to ethnic conflicts in a state not renown for racial tolerance. In the shipyards of the Bay Area, black workers felt the sting of racial discrimination. But the most serious racial incident of the war years occurred in Los Angeles in the so-called "Zoot Suit Riots" of May and June 1943. Gang violence among Latino youths, wearing garish "zoot suits," made white Angelenos begin to question the wisdom of the cultural invasion from south of the border. Called *pachucos* (Mexican slang for snappy dressers), the wearers of the flashy zoot suits became targets for service men who beat them into insensibility presumably for the pachucos' avoidance of military service. Police did nothing to stop the mob action, which the public at large tended to regard as justified retribution. White perceptions were quite inaccurate insofar as Latino patriotic service was concerned. In fact, more Latinos both volunteered for military service and won Congressional Medals of Honor proportional to their numbers than any other ethnic group during the war.

Blacks in California in Relation to Whites (In Thousands)		
Year	Blacks	Whites
1850	1	92
1860	4	323
1870	4	499
1880	6	767
1890	11	1,112
1900	11	1,403
1910	22	2,260
1920	39	3,365
1930	81	5,408
1940	124	6,597
1950	462	9,915
1960	885	14,455
1970	1,400	17,761

African Americans were a relatively small minority in California before World War II. (Data from U.S. Department of Commerce, *Historical Statistics of the United States, Colonial Times to 1970*, 2 vols., Vol. I, p. 25).

Women, blacks, Mexicans and even state convicts contributed to the state's labor force during the war. Historically, organized labor had effectively made incarceration a time of idleness for most lawbreakers. During the Depression, prisoners had often been denied the opportunity of even doing their own laundry lest they deprive some free worker of a job. Temporarily, this changed during the war. Labor shortages brought convict laborers into "harvest camps" to assist braceros. San Quentin inmates constructed commando boats, air-raid sirens, Red Cross uniforms, submarine nets, and addressed over a half billion dollars worth of ration books to the public. Convicts fought wartime forest fires with minimal guard. Morale among prisoners soared as for the first time in their lives many actually felt themselves to be useful. California's prisons led the nation in productive capacity during the war, a fact that brought Eleanor Roosevelt to San Quentin to thank the convict workers in person. With the end of the war, actual production of useful items was replaced by an empty rhetoric of rehabilitating convicts through training.

Rapid demobilization of servicemen at war's end brought additional changes. Freshly out of uniform, many ex-servicemen who had passed through California on the way to the Pacific theater found the state attractive and took up residence. New suburbs began to be carved out of heretofore undeveloped areas adjacent to the state's largest cities. Despite this activity, in the first few years after the Japanese surrender, the economy struggled with the ending of massive federal deficit spending. Then, the Cold War with the Soviet Union slowly emerged, and a new rationale for defense spending was discovered. With an increased labor force and defense plants already in place, California was well positioned for a sustained economic boom.

At the beginning of the decade, Californians had worried about their Japanese-American neighbors as potential "filth columnists," or persons liable to give aid and comfort to a foreign enemy. At the close of the forties, fear of enemies living secretly within California society continued, although communist sympathizers rather than Japanese-Americans became the new hated group. The fall of China in 1949 to the communist forces of Mao Tse-tung was inexplicable to many Americans, who assumed that only disloyalty within the American government itself could have allowed such a turn of events.

Republican Richard M. Nixon, a thirty-three-year-old navy veteran, ran for Congress in 1946 in his home district of Yorba Linda, accusing his Democratic opponent of being soft on communism. He won, as the anti-communism issue continued to gather momentum. Nixon himself gained national prominence in sending Alger Hiss, a former associate of Franklin Roosevelt, to prison. Nixon had accused Hiss of being a communist spy within the White House. While many remained skeptical of that charge, Hiss was found guilty of perjury in denying that he had ever known Whittaker Chambers, a key witness against Hiss. In 1950, California voters rewarded Nixon's anti-Communist efforts by electing him as one of their United States Senators.

Early in 1950, Wisconsin Senator Joseph McCarthy commenced his own anti-Red crusade that far outdid Richard Nixon in the kind of irresponsible allegations that came to characterize the early Cold War era. Within California, Jack B. Tenney played a role similar to that of McCarthy. From his position as Chair of a joint legislative "Fact-Finding Committee on Un-American Activities", Tenney pushed for and got the University of California Regents to enact a loyalty oath for university employees. The 1949 loyalty oath required employees to pledge that they rejected the right of revolution promised in the Declaration of Independence of 1776. Several distinguished Berkeley faculty refused to sign the required oath. They were fired. Thus, the warfare state revealed itself both at the beginning and end of the 1940s to have a low regard for traditional civil liberties.

During the late forties, the United States House of Representatives' Un-American Activities Committee investigated Hollywood's movie industry for communist influence, In an effort to minimize such external criticism, movie companies "blacklisted" actors that were suspected of holding "un-American" political beliefs. Those so labeled were effectively barred from the industry for over a decade. In this tension-filled environment, actor Ronald Reagan became President of the Screen Actors Guild. A liberal Democrat, Reagan was gradually transformed in this crucible into a popular speaker for right-wing Republican causes. This, in turn, eventually propelled him into a political career that carried him to the White House a generation later. Ironically, this graduate of California's warfare-state mentality much later undermined its very foundation. Forty years later, as President of the United States, Ronald Reagan became an active par-

ticipant in both ending the Cold War itself and any reason for continuing the warfare state.

Suggestions for Further Reading

1. Gerald D. Nash, *World War II and the West* (1990).

2. Roger W. Lotchin, *Fortress California, 1910-1961* (1992)

3. William A. Schoneberger and Paul Sonnenburg, *California Wings* (1987).

4. Roger Daniels, comp., *America's Concentration Camps* (1989).

5. Brian Masuru Hayashi, *"For the Sake of Our Japanese Brethren: "Assimilation, Nationalism, and Protestantism among the Japanese of Los Angeles, 1895-1942* (1995).

6. Paul R. Spickard, "The Nisei Assume Power: The Japanese Citizens League, 1941-1942," *Pacific Historical Review*, 52 (May 1983), 147-74.

7. Ward M. McAfee, "America's Two Japanese-American Policies During World War II," *Southern California Quarterly*, 69 (Summer 1987), 151-64.

8. Leslie T. Hatamiya, *Righting a Wrong: Japanese Americans and the Passage of the Civil Liberties Act of 1988* (1993).

9. Katherine Archibald, *Wartime Shipyard* (1947).

10. Mauricio Mazon, *The Zoot Suit Riots: The Psychology of Symbolic Annihilation* (1985).

11. Marilynn S. Johnson, *The Second Gold Rush: Oakland and the East Bay in World War II* (1994).

12. Albert S. Broussard, "Strange Territory, Familiar Leadership: The Impact of World War II on San Francisco's Black Community," *California History*, 65 (March 1986), 18-25.

13. Robert L. Allen, *The Port Chicago Mutiny: The Story of the Largest Mass Mutiny Trial in U.S. Navy History* (1989).

14. Josh Sides, "Battle on the Home Front: African American Shipyard Workers in World War II Los Angeles," *Southern California Quarterly*, 78 (Fall 1996), 250-63.

15. Otto Friedrich, *City of Nets: A Portrait of Hollywood in the 1940s* (c1986).

16. Roger E. Bilstein, *The American Aerospace Industry: From Workshop to Global Enterprise* (1996).

XVI
CALIFORNIA POLITICS GOES NATIONAL

Before the 1950s, California politicians had occasionally impacted the national scene. As an example of this, an earlier chapter focused upon the political career of Hiram Johnson and his influence on both national and global political developments during the second decade of the twentieth century. However, from the 1950s onward, California's influence upon the nation's political course has been more consistent and continuous. The state's dramatic rise to national demographic prominence, due to the booming economy of California's warfare state, produced this phenomenon.

In 1940, California had 6,907,387 people and was the nation's fifth largest state. A decade later, it had 10,586,223 inhabitants and ranked second. California flourished in the post-war baby boom, as the state's birth rate was well over twice its death rate. This ratio was much higher than the national average. In the 1960s, California bypassed even New York and became the most populous state in the Union for the first time, a status it has not lost in subsequent years. These trends could be seen most clearly as the 1950s approached. For the first time in the state's history, one aspiring California politician after another began to dream of becoming President of the United States. This was a natural consequence and a frank recognition of the state's impending preeminence.

Immediately after the Civil War, Ohio had been the ideal residential state for politicians who had presidential aspirations. Ohio was a large, industrializing state that was then most unpredictable in its political behavior. This latter factor made it politically important, even though it did not lead the nation in population. In the late nineteenth and early twentieth centuries, New York filled the role of the premier political center of the nation, due to its demographic and economic prominence. As the middle to the twentieth century approached, California stood poised to seize the honor of being the new political nesting ground of presidents.

Herbert Hoover had been the first "California president," but really Hoover had belonged to no particular state. He had been born in Iowa and was educated as an engineer at Stanford University, the primary evidence of his being a Californian. However, soon after graduation, his engineering career took him to Australia, China, Great Britain and elsewhere around the globe. He rose to national prominence in heading relief missions, first to Belgium and then to the new Soviet Union. Hoover's involvements were always global or national; for him, California only provided both a recollection of his college days and an occasional place to visit.

Earl Warren was California's first true homegrown modern presidential aspirant. Unlike Hoover, Warren built his career totally upon a California foundation. Graduating from the University of California, Warren went on to law school and then became District Attorney of Alameda County. Holding that position for thirteen years, he gained a reputation as a strong "law and order" advocate, who was characteristically tough on crime. In 1938, that identification helped him get elected as California's Attorney General. But the ambitious Warren wanted more. Also elected in 1938, Democrat Culbert Olson became California's only New Deal governor. Yet Warren could see that Olson was weak and if eventually challenged would be no match for a hard-nosed Republican with "progressive" inclinations such as himself. At the very outset of his administration, Olson was hospitalized for physical and emotional exhaustion. After that, his administration languished. Warren bided his time, sensing that soon he would be governor.

The year 1942 included a gubernatorial election, and Warren entered the race with gusto, opportunistically exploiting the public hysteria over the supposed Japanese American enemy within California's borders. While Olson vacillated on whether or not federal authorities should deprive Americans of Japanese ancestry of their civil rights, Warren showed no doubts to a cheering public. Once installed in the governor's office, Warren displayed his progressive attitudes in an unsuccessful campaign for state compulsory health insurance. Here was a Republican whom even Democrats fresh from the New Deal could applaud.

Warren was careful to placate conservative sentiment within his own party, for he needed solid Republican backing in any attempt for higher office. Accordingly, when Hiram Johnson died in 1945, Warren appointed William F. Knowland to replace him in the Senate. Knowland was the publisher of the conservative *Oakland Tribune* and the son of one of Hiram Johnson's conservative Republican enemies from the Progressive Era. Within a matter of years, Knowland himself became a conservative force in national politics. But, in the short-run, his usefulness to Warren was in keeping clear his own path to the White House.

In his bid for reelection as governor in 1946, Warren took advantage of cross-filing and ran in both the Republican and Democratic primaries, winning both, and thus demonstrating to both state and nation that here was a Republican that could win at the polls in a Democratic era. He was rewarded in 1948, when the Republican national nominating convention picked him as the vice presidential running mate of New York's Thomas Dewey. Virtually every political pundit predicted that the Dewey-Warren ticket was invincible, but President Harry Truman soon proved them wrong in one of the biggest upsets in American political history. Returning defeated to California, Warren was certain that if he, and not Dewey, had headed the Republican ticket the result would have been different.

By that time, Warren was nearing the end of his second term as governor, and no governor in California history had ever before been elected for three terms. In 1950, he accomplished this feat, which has not been matched since. And he did it by defeating Franklin Roosevelt's son, James Roosevelt. In his career up to that point, Warren appeared to be a political wonder. Not only had he won a Democratic primary as a Republican; he had defeated a Roosevelt in becoming California's only three term governor. In addition, he had been his party's faithful vice presidential standard bearer in a presidential election headed by a wooden candidate. Surely, he must have sensed that his ultimate destiny awaited fulfillment in the Republican convention of 1952.

Ohio's conservative Senator Robert Taft also dreamed of gaining the presidential prize in the convention of 1952. As the son of a president, Taft had won distinction in fighting what he regarded as the excesses of the New Deal. Subsequently, he loyally supported Roosevelt's prosecution of the war. In addition, Taft was strong in the area of civil rights, which could win the allegiance of those African Americans who still were willing to consider voting for a Republican following the Great Depression.

Nevertheless, Taft had been sidelined by Republican rivals in earlier tries for the presidency—by Wendell Wilkie in 1940 and Thomas Dewey in 1948. Warren was confident that if it came down to himself or Taft that he would come away victorious. But, as the presidential race developed, Warren's chances disintegrated. Dwight D. Eisenhower, the premier military hero of World War II and the commander of the new North Atlantic Treaty Organization, decided to enter the presidential race as a Republican and effectively stole Warren's constituency of the party's progressive wing.

Having been asked by Eleanor Roosevelt to campaign as a Democrat in 1948, Eisenhower had mostly liberal credentials entering the race in 1952. In fact, no one really knew where he stood on most issues, for as a military man he had stayed aloof from politics. Only on the eve of the campaign had he decided that he was a Republican at all. But with his entry into the race, Warren's candidacy was essentially dead, despite the latter's superb political resume.

After Eisenhower's victory over Taft in a bitter convention fight, the Republican nominee sensed the necessity of choosing a conservative running mate to salve the defeated Taft forces. Accordingly, he chose California's young Senator Richard M. Nixon. These developments galled Warren. Not only had he lost possibly his last chance at the White House, but any future hope was crushed by the selection of another Californian as Eisenhower's running mate. It was apparent to most that Eisenhower was invincible in 1952. It was equally apparent that when Eisenhower eventually vacated the White House, ambitious Richard Nixon would be his likely replacement. Nixon's popularity among a good portion of California's Republican party cast a shadow over Earl Warren's political career. Crushed, California's only three term governor went home from the convention to sulk.

As a new president, Eisenhower worked valiantly to eliminate bitterness in his own party before taking on important national and international issues. He made up with Taft, who briefly served as Eisenhower's trusted majority leader in the Senate until his death in the summer of 1953. Warren was a more difficult case. Eisenhower could see that he had unintentionally robbed Warren of his life's primary goal. The Nixon vice presidency was especially unnerving to the proud Warren. Then, on September 8, 1953, Frederick M. Vinson, the nation's Chief Justice died unexpectedly from a massive heart attack. Had he died two years later, it is unlikely that Warren would have come to the fore as a candidate for his replacement. But in the first year of Eisenhower's presidency, the office of Chief Justice made a nice peace offering to California's recently alienated governor.

Warren had absolutely no experience on the bench, but he took the position as his best of all possible options. He accepted his failure to achieve the presidency as leadership of the nation's highest court offered some potential for him to leave his mark on history.

Other frustrated presidential aspirants had become great Chief Justices--John Marshall, Samuel Chase and Charles Evans Hughes, to name a few. Warren was confident that he could outdo them all, and in the end he did.

Under his leadership, the United States Supreme Court became far more powerful than the founding fathers ever had envisioned. Ironically, he built the power of the court by leading it in directions that were diametrically opposed to those he had taken while running for and holding elective office in California. For example, he had won the governorship by exploiting white racism in 1942. In 1954, he orchestrated a unanimous court to deliver a stunning blow to long standing racist traditions in *Brown v. Education*. As Alameda's district attorney and later as California's Attorney General, he had won a reputation as a strong voice for prosecutorial justice. Later, in a series of Supreme Court cases (epitomized by *Miranda v. Arizona* [1966]), he led in providing defense attorneys with new constitutional weapons. As governor, he had opposed all efforts to dismantle California's "federal plan" of legislative apportionment. As Chief Justice, he destroyed it in *Reynolds v. Sims* (1964).

The only possible explanation for this dramatic shift on so many fronts was that the course that he took on the court helped him build the power of that institution and exalt his own place in American history. Had he presided over decisions that simply maintained the constitutional status quo, he knew that he would later become as forgotten as Fred Vinson. At the end of his career, Warren could rest satisfied that he had made a far greater impact upon American life than had Eisenhower, the man who had stolen his life's consuming ambition in the Republican nominating convention of 1952. Nevertheless, despite all of this success, one of his last official acts as Chief Justice must have been particularly irritating to the proud Californian, as it was he who swore in California's Richard M. Nixon as President of the United States on January 20, 1969.

Nixon's road to the White House was not as smooth as he had hoped following Eisenhower's landslide victory of 1952. Periodically, it was his native state of California that repeatedly proved his most serious stumbling block. In both 1958 and 1962, he was threatened with losing the very California constituency he needed for warranting a chance at the nation's highest office. Ironically, his first California challenge did not come from the friends of Earl Warren, but rather from those of conservative William F. Knowland.

Following his appointment by Governor Warren, Knowland had been elected to the Senate in his own right. Following Taft's death, Knowland had taken over the leadership of the Republican forces in the Senate; and in the fifties, he became alternatively both the majority and minority leader of that body. In such an important leadership role, he too was bitten by the presidential bug. As a political leader from California, which by then was on the threshold of becoming the premier state in the Union, Knowland knew that he had a chance for the presidency.

In the 1950s, folk wisdom held that a U.S. Senator could not run for the nation's highest executive office and win. Taft had simply been the most recent Senatorial failure. Ironically, Massachusetts Senator John F. Kennedy would trample this assumption by defeating Vice President Richard M. Nixon for the presidency in 1960. But that lay in the future, and Knowland concluded in 1958 that his chances to foil Nixon's lock on the Republican nomination in 1960 would be better if he himself first ran for governor of California and won. From that executive office, Knowland believed he could strengthen his own favorite son candidacy for the White House in 1960 and thus dash Nixon's presidential hopes, much as Nixon himself had ended Warren's chances in 1952. California was the right state for a national leader to call home, but it had room only for one favorite son.

To work his plan, Knowland first muscled California's incumbent governor, Republican Goodwin J. Knight, to run for Knowland's own senatorial seat at the same time that Knowland ran for Knight's governor's chair. This forced game of musical chairs did not present Knowland well to California's voters who sensed that ugly power politics underlay Knight's decision to go along with Knowland's wishes. Democrats saw their opportunity in the political confusion created by Knowland's overweening ambition and mounted a well organized campaign to elect Attorney General Edmund G. (Pat) Brown governor of California. The latter succeeded, silently aided by Richard Nixon's Republican friends who refused to help Knowland, who in turn intended to ruin Nixon's own presidential chances. Thus, Pat Brown became the first Democrat to be elected governor of the state in twenty years.

One of Brown's first acts as California's new governor was to wage a successful campaign to end cross-filing, a political practice which had allowed Republicans to disrupt and confuse Democratic primary campaigns. After its demise, Democrats were hopeful that their numerical superiority among the state's registered voters would begin to translate into dominance at the polls. But the subsequent record has shown that California Democrats remain an unpredictable lot and are still more likely to help elect a Republican governor of California than insure a Democratic victory through party solidarity. Since the end of cross-filing, up until the summer of 1998 when this book was completed, the only other Democrat to be elected California's governor besides Pat Brown himself has been his son Edmund G. (Jerry) Brown, Jr. In the 1990s, Californians chose yet again to blur partisan boundaries in their manner of running the direct primary process. By means of the initiative process, California now has the "blanket" primary, which allows voters of any party registration to vote for candidates across party boundaries, with all parties' nominees appearing on a single ballot. This system was first implemented in the 1998 June primary and reflects California's long heritage of remodeling the party nomination process in hopes of diminishing partisan identities.

Pat Brown's defeat of Knowland left a clear presidential field for Nixon in the 1960 Republican national convention. In the end, Nixon lost the general election in a frustratingly close presidential race to John F. Kennedy. Nixon knew that Kennedy ostensibly won only due to election fraud in Chicago and Texas, yet he chose not to challenge the result as it would have thoroughly disrupted the business of governing the nation. An official investigation also would have made him appear to be a poor loser in the eyes of many voters. Nevertheless, Nixon paid a personal cost for remaining silent. This public act of stoic defeat secretly increased his already existing paranoia, which would be amply revealed to all following his next political loss in his home state of California.

Nixon realized that his presidential defeat in 1960 necessitated his return to California to win high political office there before returning to the national spotlight. His strategy called for him to challenge Pat Brown for the gubernatorial chair in 1962. His estimate of Brown was low. Nixon had carried California against the charismatic Kennedy in 1960; certainly, he reasoned, he could defeat the lackluster Brown on the same ground.

During his first term, Brown appeared to lose part of his own liberal constituency by vacillating on the scheduled execution of convicted kidnapper Caryl Chessman at San Quentin in 1960. At first, Brown stayed the execution, but then allowed it to take place. Many opponents of capital punishment could not forgive Brown, who himself claimed to share a strong personal animus against killing prisoners while feeling bound by the clear intent of the law, which called for the termination of capital offenders. Politically weakened by the Chessman affair, Brown appeared most vulnerable.

Entering the governor's race in 1960, Nixon portrayed Brown as a minor hack in John Kennedy's national Democratic machine and ostensibly ran against the president rather than Brown himself. Both Kennedy's perceived errors in the failed Bay of Pigs invasion of Cuba and the young President's supposed weakness in allowing the Soviet Union to construct a wall around East Berlin to keep its residents from escaping to the West were well known. These events had transpired far from California; but by 1962, the state's politics could be understood clearly only in a broader perspective that included the world of foreign affairs, which candidate Nixon loved first and foremost. He obviously intended to use a victory against Brown to reenter presidential politics where he could again run against Kennedy directly.

In his first term, Brown had orchestrated an overhauling of the state master plan of higher education, which called for the construction of many new public colleges to serve the up-and-coming "baby-boom" generation. In addition, he worked hard to develop the state's burgeoning freeway system, succeeding in getting the state legislature to approve a twenty-year program of construction. Nor did his accomplishments include only new colleges and new freeways. His California State Water Project promised to deliver water from the northern part of the state to thirsty central and southern California. This plan called for the construction of the 444-mile-long California Aqueduct, branch aqueducts, 20 dams and reservoirs, 17 pumping stations and five power plants. Looking back upon the governorship of Edmund G. Brown, Sr., he truly appears to be one of the most active governors in the history of the state. But at the time of his 1962 reelection bid, neither his higher education and freeway expansion plans nor his water development blueprints had materialized into physical accomplishments that could be fully appreciated by the voting public. All that appeared before the voters was a rather bland personality, whom liberals remembered had executed Caryl Chessman and conservatives considered a Kennedy ally.

SOUTHERN CALIFORNIA'S WATER SUPPLY

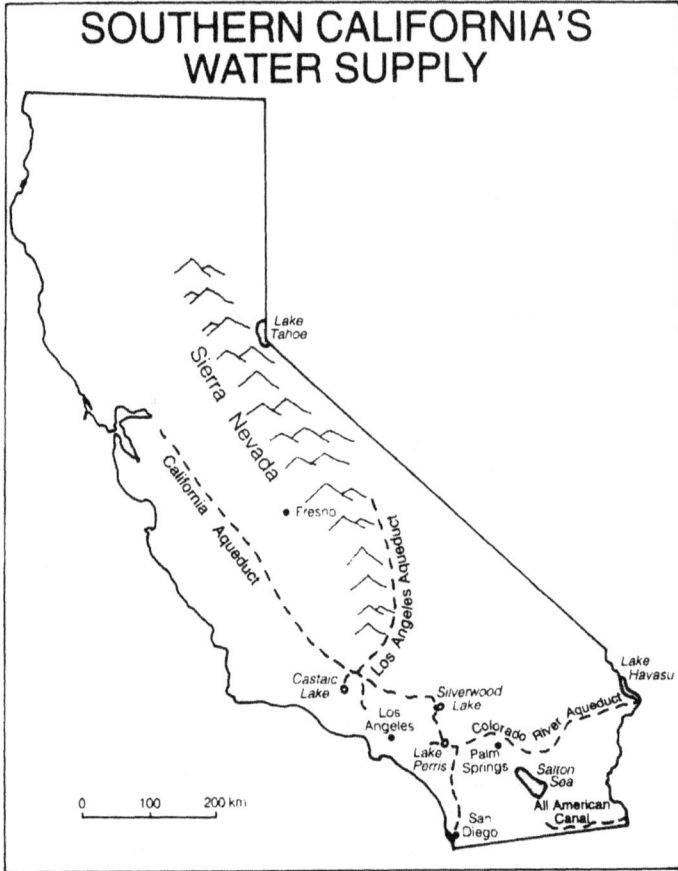

Governor Pat Brown oversaw the completion of the mixed local-state-federal de-
livery system supplying southern California with water.

Nixon's election as governor seemed assured. Then came the
Cuban Missile Crisis days before the California election. Americans
spent a string of sleepless nights, anticipating the onset of nuclear
war. As Russian ships headed for Cuba surrounded by an American
naval blockade, it was evident that for the peace of the world either
President John Kennedy or Soviet Premier Nikita Khrushchev would
have to give way. Kennedy had backed down at the Bay of Pigs and
later over the Berlin wall as well, but in this instance he held firm,

and the Soviet Union suffered a foreign-policy humiliation of the highest magnitude. The entire world breathed a collective sigh of relief as Kennedy's popularly soared as never before.

California's voters were in an especially good position to give their national commander-in-chief a vote of confidence. Voter turn-out was unusually large in the gubernatorial election of 1962. Seventy-eight percent of the electorate went to the polls and defeated the president's principal political rival by a 300,000 vote margin. Years later, reflecting upon his stunning loss to Brown, Nixon must have privately mused about the cleverness of Kennedy's precise timing in triggering this international incident. But immediately following the event, the former Vice President was not this emotionally detached. In 1960, he had quietly accepted his loss to the wily Kennedy. But the defeat in 1962 was another matter. Accordingly, he held a "last press conference" and petulantly blamed enemies in the media for his devastating defeat.

For at least a year thereafter, it appeared that Nixon had permanently retired from public life. Then, President Kennedy was murdered in Dallas, and Richard Nixon was slowly resurrected politically. Anyone whose name was so closely identified with the martyred Kennedy was again a hot political property. In 1968, following the assassination of Robert Kennedy in Los Angeles, Richard Nixon eventually won the presidency of the United States and became California's only native son to date to achieve that high office.

Ronald Reagan, who defeated Pat Brown in the latter's own bid for a third term as California's governor in 1966, eventually went on to win the White House in 1980. Reagan had been born and raised in Illinois, but as an adult moved to California, where he became a famous movie actor before challenging Brown. Reagan became California's third president. Given California's demographic dominance in the nation since 1965, more California presidents are likely in the future. Since the 1950s, the state has regularly spawned national leaders. Being from California is certainly no guarantee for national high office, but it is clearly an advantage.

Suggestions for Further Reading

1. G. Edward White, *Earl Warren, A Public Life* (1982).

2. Fawn McKay Brodie, *Richard Nixon, The Shaping of his Character* (1981).

3. Jackson K. Putnam, *Modern California Politics, 1917-1980* (1980).

4. K. Schuparra, "Freedom vs. Tyranny—The 1958 California Election and the Origins of the State's Conservative Movement," *Pacific Historical Review*, 63 (Nov.1994), 537-60.

5. Totton J. Anderson, "The 1958 Election in California," *Western Political Quarterly*, 12 (March 1959), 276-300.

6. Roger Rapoport, *California Dreaming: The Political Odyssey of Pat and Jerry Brown* (1982).

7. Harvey P. Grody, "From North to South: The Feather River Project and Other Legislative Water Struggles in the 1950s," *Southern California Quarterly*, 60 (Fall 1978), 287-323.

XVII
CALIFORNIA DREAMING

If the 1950s proved to be the decade when California emerged as the nation's future political center, the following decade made the state the cultural capital as well. In this respect, no suggestion is intended that any California metropolis has by-passed New York City as the premier center of American high society. California's claim to cultural dominance occurred at more plebian levels in the arena commonly known as popular culture. In this mass audience, California's dreams and fantasies have certainly been uppermost since the raucous decade of the sixties. As shown in an earlier chapter, California's global influence in image-making was obvious even in the 1920s due to the influence of Hollywood. But that was restrained compared to that which became evident in the sixties and afterward.

The demographic revolution popularly known as the post-war "Baby Boom" had much to do with this dramatic cultural change. American culture has always favored "new" over "old" and youthful exuberance over the reflective wisdom of advanced age. Accordingly, young California in the 1960s grabbed the nation's attention. Whatever young Californians did in that decade seemed to hypnotize wider audiences. Baby boomers from all over the United States wanted to go to California, for they sensed that there, as nowhere else, a new way of living and being was evolving.

The force of tradition was weaker in California than elsewhere. Personal freedom was greater in California than elsewhere. Opportunities were more varied in California than elsewhere. None of this was new. It could have been said of the state in 1850 or 1900, as well as 1960. But in the 1960s, the California dream took on a new, more vibrant image. Experimental attitudes involving both sexuality and drug use embraced California's easy-going tradition of having no traditions. A veritable popular-culture hothouse resulted that has characterized California in the latter part of the twentieth century.

"The Pill" played a large role in this cultural transformation. It liberated young women from the fear of unwanted pregnancy and spawned a revolution in sexual pleasure-making. The "sun and surf" of the "California Riviera" along the long coastline from Pismo Beach in the north to Coronado in the south encouraged this sexual revolution. Young women, publicly revealing their physical charms in "bikinis," suggested in the minds of the young men who admired them that self-restraint had clearly been discarded. "Have you done 'it' yet?" became a leading question for pubescent girls. In this happy environment of warm sun and warmer skin, few wished to appear old fashioned. But, youthful conformity took a toll. As the social velocity of the decade increased, evidence of the consequences of never saying "no" began to accumulate. By the end of the decade, the youth-culture's "California dream" often appeared, even to the Baby Boomer experimenters themselves, as a California nightmare.

Hollywood played a leading role in this cultural revolution. Challenged by sexually explicit foreign films after World War II, California's film industry abandoned the self-censorship that had characterized it from the early 1920s. Here too, self-restraint dissolved in the 1960s. Predictably, some parents, recoiling from suggestive advertisements luring their children into movie houses, put an "Anti-Smut" initiative on the California ballot in 1966, threatening to bring Hollywood under state censorship. On the federal level, the Warren Court was then applying First Amendment freedoms through the Fourteenth Amendment to restrict state policing of public morals, so the initiative's possible unconstitutionality was identified by its opponents.

Ironically, the clinching opposition to censoring Hollywood came from conservative Ronald Reagan, former President of the Screen Actors Guild, who was running against Pat Brown for governor of the state in that same year. Reagan calmed concerned parents by suggesting that Hollywood was about to install a new mode of self-policing and that they need not resort to such a radical instrument as state censorship. Accordingly, the initiative failed. Hollywood then instituted a rating system informing parents of the nature of the films being shown in the public market. It was a form of self-policing that completely avoided issues of censorship. And the cultural revolution proceeded unchecked.

As the decade progressed, a new term entered the American lexicon—"the generation gap." The Baby Boom generation predominated on one side of this divide. It was "liberated," tolerant of different cultural "lifestyles" and morally self-righteous about the racial bigotry of older Americans. On the other side were "uptight" parents, "unaware" of how their own lives had been "repressed" in meeting the expectations of others, and very nervous about their children listening to a new music named "rock 'n roll."

The generation gap entered into every spectrum of life, including politics. Young whites not only listened and danced to black-
inspired music, they also increasingly sympathized with a civil-rights
movement for black liberation from historic white oppression. This
latter aspect of the generation gap most profoundly entered the
American consciousness by events occurring on the Berkeley campus
of the University of California in the autumn of 1964.

White baby boomers at Berkeley had been inspired by the
youth-oriented presidency of John F. Kennedy. Many had signed up
for his Peace Corps in hopes that they could improve the world in
some small way. His assassination in the autumn of 1963 left them
temporarily abandoned in their idealism, and many of them gravitated
to more dangerous avenues to test their moral mettle. In their minds,
Kennedy had given his life for opposing hateful traditions. Multiple
speculations of sinister forces engineering the president's killing further spurred them to action. In the summer of 1964, many Berkeley
students ventured into the South to work at the grass-roots of the civil
rights movement. There they encountered directly the ugly and violent tradition of Jim Crow. As battle-seasoned veterans of angry confrontations, these students returned to campus in the fall with a purpose to fight the enemies of civil rights in their own neighborhoods.
William Knowland's conservative *Oakland Tribune* opposed both
Martin Luther King's strategy and tactics. Accordingly, students
mounted on-campus organizing efforts to shut down the newspaper
with massive sit-ins.

Knowland, who had retired from politics following his defeat for governor in 1958, contacted friends on the University Board
of Regents and complained that a public university should not be used
as a staging ground for partisan activities. This concern filtered down
to the administration of the campus, which quickly installed restrictions on political speech and organizing on campus. Suddenly, the
focus of the student's organizing changed. The *Oakland Tribune*
faded as the locus of their rage. They became aware of an even closer
enemy--the U.C. administration itself. In this way, the Berkeley Free
Speech Movement of 1964 was born.

A charismatic student orator by the name of Mario Savio
held masses of students spellbound. He called for sit-ins, was arrested, and became an instant hero to the students hungering for leadership. Police were repeatedly brought on to campus, as a battle of
wills between students and administrators raged for months. Ameri-

can society had never seen anything like it before. News photos of the Berkeley confrontations seemed menacingly foreign. In only a few years, they would seem mild and tame, for that which followed in the late sixties was far more violent and ugly.

A slogan came out of the Berkeley Free Speech Movement (FSM) of that autumn that captured the spirit of a rising youth rebellion: "Don't trust anyone over thirty." An initiative on the California ballot that fall reflected the growing generation gap on issues involving race. Proposition 14 called for the repeal of California's Rumford Fair Housing Act, a measure that had been passed by the state legislature to insure fair treatment in real estate dealings. Under the Rumford Act, conservative critics claimed, private-property rights were compromised in the name of civil rights. White property owners, fearful of a decline in property values in transitional neighborhoods, tended to favor the initiative. By contrast, "No on 14" bumper stickers predominated on the Berkeley campus. When Proposition 14 was enacted by more than a million vote margin, FSM students believed more than ever that they could not trust anyone over thirty. Ultimately, the courts overturned the proposition as in violation of the U.S. Constitution's Fourteenth Amendment; but by then it was too late. The polarizing impact of Proposition 14 had already occurred.

The following August, young blacks took to the streets of the Watts area of Los Angeles in a bloody week-long riot that became the greatest urban disturbance of the twentieth century up to that point. Just as "No on 14" bumper stickers had predominated in Berkeley the autumn before, "Yes on 14" banners had typically been favored by white Angelenos. In effect, this slogan told blacks that they were not wanted in California. With the end of the wartime employment boom, black unskilled labor had not stopped coming to California from the Deep South. After the war, many African Americans had not been able to find work. As the automatic cotton-picking machine eliminated employment opportunities in their states of origin, mechanized trenchers and other new machines dried up traditional outlets for unskilled labor where they ultimately landed.

In deep despair, many blacks became virtual permanent wards of the state, as families broke up to enable abandoned wives and children to receive public assistance. No meaningful opportunities for self improvement were available, as the African American newcomers sunk into the hopelessness of idleness and uselessness. Berkeley's students had gone into the South to battle racial injustice, but here in their own state a racial problem was festering with no easy answers. The black newcomers sensed disgust and condemnation on white faces wherever they went. In Los Angeles, it was especially apparent.

Pattern For Chaos

A hopelessness fed by joblessness insured that the rioting of 1965 would likely come again. (Cartoon by Newton Pratt, Courtesy, *The Sacramento Bee* and Thomas Platt.)

Early in the decade, southern California musical groups such as The Beach Boys and Jan and Dean established what came to be known as the California Sound. It was oriented to sun, surf, tanned bodies, fast cars and above all the material concerns of white middle-class youth. This new sound was as close as rock 'n roll came to being "white." The music was not intentionally racist, but the image of southern California imparted in the lyrics of their songs had no place for non-whites. It celebrated a disappearing ethnic homogeneity that largely had typified southern California since the Health Rush of the late nineteenth century. The blond athlete of Venice pier, the tanned "surf hon" of Zuma beach—these were the folk heroes of the California Sound.

In the Watts Riots of 1965, black youth announced their disturbing presence on the scene. "Burn, baby, burn," was their chant as they torched stores already gutted by looters. "Kill the white man," the youthful rioters vented, as white Angelenos went to local gun shops to equip themselves for an anticipated racial Armageddon. The national guard was brought in to restore a superficial peace, but both blacks and whites knew that true peace would be a long time coming.

Nothing like the Berkeley Free Speech Movement had ever happened in the United States before. Nothing on the scale of the Watts Riots had ever happened in the United States before. By the end of the decade, that which had happened first at Berkeley and Watts would be commonplace all across the American landscape. These two events proved a fundamental cultural reality that continues to hold true. If any deep-seated cultural changes occur in modern American society, they usually first make themselves visible in California.

After the Watts Riots, the generation gap only deepened. Those over thirty elected Ronald Reagan governor in 1966. Pat Brown was blamed for failing to prevent both the Berkeley Free Speech Movement and the Watts Riots. Both events were substantially beyond his control, but Brown was criticized anyway. Newly installed Governor Reagan implied by his tough talk that no such nonsense would be tolerated while he was governor. Trouble occurred anyway. Berkeley continued to fester as a hot bed of upheaval over both perceived social injustices and growing opposition to the war in Vietnam. Black rage continued unabated, characterized by the emergence of the Black Panthers out of Oakland's black ghetto. In the year of Reagan's election, Bobby Seale and Huey Newton founded the organization devoted to terrorizing white police with the same methods that the latter historically had used to keep blacks under control. The Panthers wore their own uniforms, toted riffles and trailed police cars patrolling their neighborhoods. Eldridge Cleaver, a convicted rapist, became the Black Panther Minister of Information and wrote a best-selling book entitled *Soul on Ice* (1968). Young white college students read it, wanting to understand Cleaver's rage. Reagan and the older generation that had elected him could do nothing about this. And the gap widened.

More than any other part of the United States, the San Francisco Bay Area became the national center of a counter culture arising out of white baby-boomer yearnings to relate to those who had been oppressed by their elders. San Francisco had long been associated with an easy tolerance towards divergent life styles. Jack Kerouac and his Beatniks had found a ready home in the city a decade before. Historically, San Francisco prided itself on harboring eccentrics. "Emperor Norton," a bankrupted merchant who had proclaimed himself emperor of San Francisco, had been humored by the city during the generation after the Gold Rush. Such antics were part of San Francisco's charm. Taking advantage of this acceptance, youthful experimenters termed "hippies" flocked to the city's Haight-Ashbury district in 1966 and 1967 as a new American popular culture took form.

LSD (or "acid") was the drug of choice in "the Haight." It was promoted as "mind-expanding," but after a few years of observing the effects of its indiscriminate use among late adolescents, "mind-destroying" seemed a more apt description. As southern California had earlier generated the "California Sound," San Francisco's The Grateful Dead and The Jefferson Airplane made "Acid Rock" world famous. As the decibels of the music increased at the end of the decade, the generation gap became a chasm. Violence in a student/faculty strike at San Francisco State in the winter of 1968-1969, as well as across the bay at "People's Park" (a piece of University of California property expropriated by hippies living on Berkeley's streets) disturbed thoughtful Californians who feared the unraveling of their society.

"Altamont" proved to wake up a large segment of the Bay Area's hippie counterculture to dangers inherent in creating their brave new world of no restraints. "Altamont" started innocently enough. The British rock group The Rolling Stones had wanted to perform in San Francisco's Golden Gate Park at the close of the decade but had been unable to secure a permit. Accordingly, they held their concert on December 6, 1969, at Altamont across the bay, in a large field near Livermore. Hells Angels from Los Angeles were hired by the "Stones" for "security." This turned out to be a fatal mistake, as those commissioned to keep order terrorized both performers and the audience near the stage. In the end, only one young man was killed in the affair, but his lonely death cast a pall across the entire decade. California dreaming had turned into a twisted odyssey that even frightened some of its most ardent supporters. U.C. Berkeley's student newspaper termed the event "the end of a decade of dreams."

However, the decade was not a loss. American popular culture had experimented with new frontiers of sexuality, racial tolerance and ways of living and being. Few who shared the experience from beginning to end were not transformed in some way by the process. At one extreme were the hippies themselves. At the other, San Francisco State's famed semanticist, S.I. Hayakawa, was changed from a tolerant academician into a rigid cultural icon of political conservatives. Emerging as the president of the university, Hayakawa physically confronted student radicals during the strike of 1968-69 by tearing wires out of their sound truck, thus temporarily silencing them. In the following decade, he was rewarded by being elected California's first and only (to date) Japanese-American United States Senator. For Californians to elect an Asian American to such a high office gave evidence that the voters of the state had at least partially undermined one significant prejudice from their past.

Asian/Pacific Islander Population The Top Five States In Rank Order, 1980 and 1990				
	1990		1980	
State	Population	% of State Total	Population	% of State Total
California	2,845,659	9.6	1,253,818	5.3
New York	693,760	3.9	310,526	1.8
Hawaii	685,236	61.8	583,252	60.5
Texas	319,459	1.9	120,313	0.8
Illinois	285,311	2.5	159,653	1.4

Information taken from Susan Gall and Irene Natividad, eds., *The Asian American Almanac* (Gale Research Inc.: Detroit, 1995), p. 286.

Californians of Hispanic culture were also transformed in the decade. Observing the battles between blacks and whites, young Chicanos were moved to redefine their own place in California's evolving ethno-cultural landscape. While often appearing to imitate the actions of African-American innovators (i.e., the Chicanos' Brown Berets followed the creation of the Black Panthers), Latinos began to grow in self-consciousness at the close of the decade. The emergence of Cesar Chavez as the principal cultural hero of California's Latino community addressed a deep-seated need among a minority long marginalized in California history. As head of the United Farm Workers, Chavez led a movement to improve the lot of agricultural labor, which historically had existed at sub-human levels in California. In 1966, he led a 300-mile march from Delano in the San Joaquin valley to Sacramento to publicize "huelga," a strike against powerful growers. By itself, that event made Chavez a national figure, occupying for Chicanos the role of the saintly revolutionary, similar to that held by Martin Luther King, Jr., in the African-American consciousness.

The women's movement likewise took inspiration from black trailblazers. In the following decade, California women joined with their sisters in other states to explore the parameters of feminism. Thereafter, male/female relationships were permanently altered. Through it all, African Americans remained the pioneers in attempting to develop a new multicultural America. Their unique history of being virtual perpetual outcasts in their native land gave them revolutionary credentials that could be matched by no other group. And always, their struggle seemed to come back to California for landmark developments.

"Affirmative Action" was a concept that was first applied to blacks and eventually to all other "underrepresented minorities" (i.e., Latinos, women, Native Americans, among others). The concept evolved out of a realization of the late sixties that de facto discrimination (the prejudice that lives in individual hearts) can be just as restrictive as de jure discrimination (racial separatism that is built into law). The sixties had effectively dismantled de jure segregation, but de facto separatism had barely been scratched. And so, new governmental programs were designed to help ensure that persons victimized by historic patterns of discrimination were allotted advantageous considerations. Some argued that quotas should be established, guaranteeing specific groups admission into colleges or professional schools up to certain percentages of available openings. The same logic applied to hiring. Others cautioned that quotas merely amounted to reverse discrimination and that affirmative action should be finessed rather than forced. This latter understanding prevailed in

Bakke v. U.C. Regents (1978), a U.S. Supreme Court case involving the medical school at U.C. Davis.

The Bakke decision ruled that in Affirmative-Action admission decisions to the U.C. Davis medical school, race, gender, and other similar considerations could be considered as one set of many factors, including grades and perceived talents. However, it could not be the sole factor. Translated, this meant that Affirmative Action could not legitimately be used to hire or choose persons unfit or unqualified to serve or study in whatever specific role that might be under consideration. Nevertheless, finessing Affirmative Action often proved difficult in concrete situations, where often it appeared that quotas or set asides were in fact operational, despite official promises to the contrary.

Emerging from the upheavals of the sixties, persons of good will continued to wrestle with issues that surfaced in that revolutionary time. In some aspects, the decade was a birthing time, as many positive efforts to improve society began then. Ancient evils involving racial discrimination came under siege, but new evils surfaced in the decade as well.

The face of death could be seen in the strange gaze of Charles Manson, who led his "family" in an orgy of killing in Los Angeles in 1969. Hollywood actress Sharon Tate, four of her houseguests, as well as a Los Angeles grocer and his wife in a separate incident, served as victims for their blood lust. As graduates of Haight-Ashbury's unrestricted hippie counterculture, Manson's family lived by whatever whim came into their charismatic leader's twisted mind. Manson and three of his followers were convicted of murder, reminders of the malignant underside of the liberated sixties.

The same ugly aspect of the decade infected the Symbionese Liberation Army (S.L.A.), an East Bay group of self-appointed freedom fighters that assassinated Oakland Superintendent of Schools Marcus Foster in 1973. Foster's "crime" had been his resolve to maintain order in his city's schools. However, this murder did not succeed in bringing the S.L.A. fame. That came in the following year, when the organization kidnapped (and later recruited) Patty Hearst, granddaughter of William Randolph Hearst. For the next two years, the law-breaking escapades of the group and their heiress convert (renamed "Tania") became a major media event of the seventies. Eventually, most of the gang was killed in a shootout with Los Angeles police. "Tania" remained at bay until 1975, but eventually Patty

Hearst was tried and convicted, and in 1979 was released by a presidential pardon. This episode blended many elements of the sixties' revolutionary ideology—multi-cultural visions of an ideal America led by youth rejecting conventional standards of right and wrong and characterized by personality changes of major and destructive proportions.

Both the Manson Family and the S.L.A. were extreme products of their time, but they also evidenced a cultural problem lingering from the decade's celebration of personal liberation. Serious questions from the sixties remain as the California dream continues. In a free society, what constitutes legitimate limits of individual expression? Does personal freedom have any boundaries required for the maintenance of liberty? Are there any absolute standards of right and wrong in a healthy democratic society? The answers Californians give to these questions in the twenty-first century will define not only their own state's future but that of the United States as well, as California continues to remain a cultural trend setter.

Suggestions for Further Reading

1. Anthony Fawcett, *California Rock, California Sound* (1979).

2. Jack McDonough, *San Francisco Rock* (1985).

3. Timothy Miller, *The Hippies and American Values* (1991).

4. Lawrence Paul Crouchett, "Assemblyman W. Byron Rumford, Symbol for an Era," *California History*, 66 (March 1987), 12-23.

5. David Lance Goines, *The Free Speech Movement: Coming of Age in the 1960s* (1989).

6. W.J. Rorabough, *Berkeley at War: The 1960s* (1989).

7. Raphael J. Sonenshein, *Politics in Black and White: Race and Power in Los Angeles* (1993).

8. Gerald Home, *Fire This Time: The Watts Uprising and the 1960s* (1995).

9. Henry P. Anderson, *The Bracero Program in California* (1976).

10. Richard Griswold del Castillo and Richard A. Garcia, *Cesar Chavez: A Triumph of Spirit* (1995).

11. Carlos Muñoz, *Youth, Identity, Power: The Chicano Movement* (1990).

12. Gary C. Hamilton and Nicole Woolsey Biggart, *Governor Reagan, Governor Brown* (1984).

13. Gerald J. De Groot, "Ronald Reagan and Student Unrest in California, 1966-1970," *Pacific Historical Review*, 65 (February 1996), 107-129.

XVIII
THE AGE OF LIMITS

Compared with the 1960s, the decade of the seventies was characterized by limits and boundaries. The sixties had been an age of excess. That decade had begun with an ethos that anything was possible. "Automation," a word that envisioned a future of computer-run robots doing the work of society, had promised to open new vistas for personal freedom and exploration. The nation's young president had pledged that the sixties would not end before a man walked on the moon. And, by the end of the decade, that came true. In the sixties, many reached for the stars. But, by the time that American astronauts landed on the moon, Americans had grown disenchanted with the excesses of their time. As the 1970s began, the public yearned for less dynamic change.

Lyndon Johnson had been the quintessential politician of the sixties. For him, everything was possible. He had waged a costly war in Vietnam, while at the same time undertaking his "Great Society" reforms to bring about social justice at home. While some warned that the national budget would be broken by both "guns and butter" simultaneously, the ebullient Johnson roared ahead, confident that history would vindicate his bold choices. In contrast, California's Governor Ronald Reagan called for limited government, even while his state boomed economically. The conservative governor's rhetorical stances were not often translated into stark policy changes. California's public works continued to multiply, even under Reagan. As his predecessor's water projects and new university campuses materialized, expansion of state government was inevitable. Nevertheless, Reagan vowed to "cut the fat out of the system" of this growing government, and the voters approved by reelecting him in 1970.

As the decade of the seventies began, California's Richard Nixon sat in the White House, pledged to bring an end to the unpopular Vietnam War. But in the spirit of his predecessor, he found it necessary to expand the war in order to create an opportunity to negotiate a peace. His invasion of Cambodia in 1970 sparked fresh academic protests that led to the temporary closure of many California universities. Breaking the sixties' habits of excess proved to be as difficult for governmental policy makers as it was for that decade's heroin addicts.

The gunning down of young people at Kent State in 1970, which occurred in the aftermath of the Cambodia invasion, cautioned radical students that their behavior might lead to their deaths. After an initial wave of anger over Kent State passed, university students, both in California and elsewhere, became more subdued. Nixon's subsequent ending of the military draft and the creation of an all volunteer army contributed to this new mood as well. University campuses during the 1970s were placid when compared to the sixties.

Nixon's response to the Arab-Israeli Yom Kippur War of 1973 indirectly encouraged a decade of limits. In that war, the Israelis were surprised by a coordinated Egyptian/Syrian attack on their High Holy Day. Israel's Arab enemies had long called for destroying the Zionist state, and early in that conflict that appeared to be a distinct possibility. President Nixon responded decisively, aggressively re-supplying the Israeli forces in their darkest hour, enabling them to recover and eventually retake lost ground. Had not the Soviet Union threatened world war, the American-strengthened Israelis might have totally vanquished their enemies.

The Arab world viewed Nixon's aid to Israel as excessive and rushed to punish the United States for its interference. Arab nations wanted to teach average Americans that negative consequences could result from their uncritical acceptance of their government's unabashedly pro-Israeli foreign policy. Such was the background of the Arab Oil Embargo that began in 1973. This action lasted for five months, but when the embargo ended, higher prices for oil were maintained by O.P.E.C., the Organization of Petroleum Exporting Countries. For the rest of the decade, the American economy experienced new and unwanted restrictions and limitations.

California was especially hard hit by this international development. More than any other state, California was dependent upon automobile transportation. Gas shortages severely impacted California commuters. Used to their personal freedom, Californians had to adjust suddenly to unwanted car pooling in order to get to work. Having reached new heights of instant gratification in the previous decade, Californians found long gas lines a hard lesson. Nixon proclaimed a new speed limit of 55 miles per hour as part of a national effort to conserve fuel. Seemingly overnight, the American people were being forced to slow down. For Californians who were pioneering a new, fast and mobile lifestyle, this development was exceptionally difficult.

An age of limits came also in response to Nixon's "imperial presidency." The nation's Watergate crisis, brought about by Nixon's

excesses in conducting espionage against his domestic enemies, produced a national backlash against governmental arrogance and abuse
of power. Congressional investigation of his mode of executive operations eventually led to his resignation from the presidency on August 9, 1974. Nixon then retreated into exile within the compound of
his "Western White House" at San Clemente, as fallout from the first
presidential resignation in American history clouded the political
landscape.

Ronald Reagan had been a popular two-term governor, but
even he chose not to face the possibility of the voters' anti-Watergate
mood turning on him should he try for a third term in 1974. Californians had long regarded three gubernatorial terms as excessive. In all
of California history, only Earl Warren successfully breached that
political boundary. A politically wise Ronald Reagan decided not to
take the chance as the Watergate crisis temporarily stained excessive
political behavior in general and that of his own party in particular.
Reagan had presidential aspirations that he did not want to put at risk
in 1974. The fact that he would be a former governor of the nation's
largest state, together with his continuing celebrity status, guaranteed
his prominence before the public eye even after he left Sacramento.
He did not need a third term to keep his political options open.

Reagan's temporary departure from government cleared the
stage for the Democratic nominee for governor that year—Jerry
Brown, son of Pat Brown. The son was radically different from his
father. Whereas Pat Brown had the demeanor of a businessman interested in economic development, Jerry Brown's personality was that of
a brash spiritual seeker characterized by frequent sophomoric pronouncements. At one point in his life, the younger Brown had trained
for the Roman Catholic priesthood, but eventually opted out of pursu-
ing so restrictive a calling. Instead, he investigated Zen Buddhism,
which he found more appealing. A philosophy major in college, Jerry
Brown loved to muse about ideas in public. In contrast, his father had
been a most down-to-earth and practical man of worldly affairs, primarily concerning himself with the economic growth of the nation's
largest state. Typical of other politicians in the sixties, Pat Brown had
thought primarily in terms of a progress that could be measured quan-
titatively. He had not worried unduly about "quality of life" issues.
He had once said that when California finally became overcrowded,
people would leave for other states as part of a natural process that
did not necessitate undue public planning. His son had a different

attitude and chose an opposite course. After being elected governor in 1974, he built his new administration around the notion of California living within restricted limits and boundaries.

Starting with Petaluma in 1973, California communities began to enact limited growth ordinances in hopes of maintaining the "quality of life" long associated with the golden state. The younger Brown achieved power at just the right moment for him. He loved to philosophize about the virtues of reducing the psychological pull of material attachments. Slow growth fit into his value orientation. At the outset of his first term, E.F. Schumacher's popular *Small Is Beautiful* (1973) called for "Buddhist economics" and a reorientation of the American economy around living simply rather than always striving for more material goods. In ancient times, the historic Buddha had preached that striving only breeds unhappiness. True contentment, he had taught, comes from actively choosing to live with less. The idea was fundamentally in violation of the so-called American way of life, which historically had promoted dynamic growth and ever rising levels of material prosperity.

But, in the early seventies, Californians were having second thoughts about mindlessly continuing this historic pattern. The causes for this change of heart were multiple, involving growth problems associated with California being the nation's most populous state and the temporary misery of long gas lines brought on by O.P.E.C. By the seventies, environmental degradation had become synonymous with "progress." In 1969 and 1971, oil spills soiled Santa Barbara beaches and San Francisco Bay respectively. In addition, the multiple hangovers of Watergate, Vietnam and the hippie excesses of the late sixties made Jerry Brown's message of rethinking the definition of "progress" refreshing, at least at the outset.

Jerry Brown refused to move into the new governor's mansion, which had been built during the Reagan years. He said that it was excessive and that all he needed was a small apartment. He refused the governor's limousine. All he needed was an old nondescript vehicle that was fully adequate to take him from place to place. The people loved this reverse of ostentatious display. Here was an elected official with seemingly none of the imperiousness that had stained the Nixon administration on the national level. Here was a simple man of the people, or so it appeared at the time.

Jerry Brown continued the limited government message of Reagan. He was against raising taxes and said that government should live within that limitation. He told state university professors, who had not received real salary increases under the parsimonious Reagan, that he too was against raising their pay. They already had, he offered, "psychic income" from the joy of teaching and researching their fields of interest. He suggested that they meditate upon this in lieu of dreaming about the material things that fatter paychecks could purchase. He also suggested to the automobile-commuting public that he would build no new freeways to relieve congestion. Instead, Adrianna Gianturco, his chief of transportation, introduced the diamond lane on California freeways to allow car pools to travel at higher rates of speed during rush-hour traffic. By encouraging car pools, Brown's administration was joining national efforts to conserve fuel, while at the same time saving both the environment and the state the costs of additional freeway construction.

The younger Brown was a liberal Democrat who superficially appeared not far from conservative Republicanism. Governing in the shadow of Watergate, Brown appeared to be a careful steward of public expenditures and an advocate of governmental self-restraint. Yet behind the scenes, Brown was also working a quiet revolution. More than any California governor before or since, he made affirmative action appointments. Women primarily benefitted from his policy. Not only was Adrianna Gianturco his CalTrans director, but he chose Rose Bird as Chief Justice of the California Supreme Court, a position from which she waged an active campaign against the state's death penalty. The governor also established a new farm labor board to advance the interests of a group that had historically been exploited by powerful interests. He also showed a greater sensitivity toward environmental issues than any California governor before or since. In these ways, Jerry Brown furthered a liberal political agenda while preaching a fiscal conservatism reminiscent of Ronald Reagan.

Brown was fond of recommending the Buddhist teaching that craving should be minimized as it inevitably leads to suffering, but ironically he himself had not fully learned this lesson. This was demonstrated at the end of the decade, when due to his fiscal conservatism, unspent tax revenues accumulated in the state treasury. By 1978, a five billion dollar state surplus had been amassed. Just as significantly, by that time, Brown's desire to run for president was in full bloom. This surplus, combined with his own craving to be president, eventually proved his undoing.

Governor Jerry Brown told Californians that they would be happier if
they lowered their expectations. Cartoonist Dennis Renault found this
advice ripe for political satire. (Courtesy, *The Sacramento Bee* and
Dennis Renault.)

The late seventies was a time both of economic stagnation
and monetary inflation, a strange combination that ran counter to the
modern American experience. Californians were in a restive mood,
feeling not only the pinch of higher fuel prices and a general inflation
that followed, but also static wages brought about by an uncertain
economy. Had Brown simply given back the mounting state surplus
to the taxpayers as it accumulated, his own political stock would have
risen and the public mood might have improved. But this he did not
do. Insiders in 1978 speculated that he planned to wait until the eve of
the presidential campaign two years later, when he would give back

the surplus with a great flourish that would capture media attention. But Californians were not willing to wait until 1980. They wanted relief immediately.

Tax reformers Howard Jarvis and Paul Gann stepped into the void created by Brown's inaction over the surplus. Through the initiative process, they placed Proposition 13 on the state ballot in 1978. It proposed to reduce property taxes significantly. Throughout the decade housing values had climbed steadily, and with them property taxes had risen. Retirees on fixed incomes, already suffering greatly from inflation, could not afford to pay the tax bills on their homes. Some were forced to sell their homes of a lifetime simply to avoid an unbearable tax burden. Jarvis and Gann broadcast such stories. The certainty that their reform would prove to be a windfall for wealthy land speculators had far less effect on a public yearning for a break in taxes.

At first, Governor Brown came out against Proposition 13 and felt the blast of public disapproval. As he himself was running in 1978 for reelection to another four-year term as governor, Brown could not afford to be on the wrong side on such a politically sensitive issue. So, he hastily switched sides and appeared with Howard Jarvis on television promoting the reform. In the short run, this move was smart politics. It enabled his re-election, as he chose not to oppose the tidal wave that soon became known as the "California Tax Revolt." But in the long run, this switch was devastating to Brown's own image as a man of political integrity.

Having to come to power in the shadow of Watergate, Brown had early appeared to be a straight-talking antidote to a lying Richard Nixon. In his early administration, everyone knew Brown's positions on the issues clearly. The younger Brown's habit of verbally "shooting from the hip" had served him well early in his political career. But after his opportunistic switch on Proposition 13, no one could be sure where he really stood. It seemed for the first time that he had become just another weasel-worded politician. Jokes were made about him. "Jerry Jarvis" became a new nickname for the governor. Suddenly, he was vulnerable. The nationally syndicated comic strip "Doonesbury" joined in the hunt and ridiculed him as "Governor Moonbeam." Rapidly, he devolved from a meaningful presidential aspirant into a cartoon character of all that was unpredictable, unconventional and unreliable in California culture. Worst of all, strategists in his own party blamed him for the California tax revolt. Had he not greedily held on to the tax surplus, they whined, the political revolt might never had occurred. As matters sorted themselves out after the passage of Proposition 13, the state surplus quickly disappeared in bailing out local governments financially strapped by the rapid erosion of their tax base. By 1980, the surplus was gone, and Jerry Brown's presidential chances disappeared with it.

Another California politician proved to be the primary beneficiary of the state's tax revolt. Ronald Reagan promised that if voters promoted his national candidacy he would take California's anti-tax sentiment into the White House itself. From there, he promised, he would lower taxes for all Americans. This dream came true as the Republican party nominated Reagan for president in 1980, and he went on to win the general election against President Jimmy Carter. Following that, Reagan made lowering taxes one of his highest priorities. The nation's leading state had spoken through direct democracy. Only a few years later, the nation itself followed California's pioneering call to cut back on government in order to make up for undesirable short falls in anticipated personal income.

By 1980, both Californians and Americans at large refused to accept Buddhist economics. They refused to let go of their desires for more material goods. If allowed to choose between maintaining governmental services and increasing personal discretionary income during a stagnant economic era, they chose the latter. Reagan promised that their choice eventually would lead to economic growth and a renewed prosperity.

Restoration of national military readiness was another high priority of President Reagan. This too was enacted into law and resulted in greatly increased federal spending in defense industries, which directly benefited economic growth in California as in no other state. Accordingly, the 1980s proved to be a time of economic boom in California. But, nationally, there was a price to be paid for the simultaneous implementation of tax cutting and increased defense spending. Ironically, the fiscally "responsible" former California governor led the nation toward an abyss of fiscal irresponsibility.

As for Jerry Brown, he continued as governor until the end of his term. Then, he ran unsuccessfully for the United States Senate. Defeated, he retreated to a voluntary exile in Japan to imbibe Zen's teachings from its most vital source. From there, he went to India, to work with Mother Teresa in helping the sick and dying. Spiritually restored, he returned to California and made another unsuccessful bid for the presidency in 1992. Six years later, the city of Oakland elected Jerry Brown as their Mayor. In this role, his political career continues beyond the publication date of this volume.

Ronald Reagan had earlier wrestled with his own demons of ambition when he had tried to unseat Gerald Ford in the Republican national convention of 1976. The contest for the Republican nomination for the presidency that year was a tight one, despite the fact that Ford, as the President of the United States, had far more resources to insure his own nomination than Reagan. At that time, Reagan felt that he had no choice other than to challenge a sitting president, as he was then 65 years of age and his future opportunities to seek the office were limited. In the short run, he lost. Reagan took this defeat in the convention gracefully and campaigned for Ford in the general election. Some of his followers wanted to make him the champion of a third party effort, but he refused to cooperate. Reagan's party loyalty following his loss to Ford eventually reaped him beneficial returns. Ford lost that election, clearing the field in 1980 for an aging but ultimately victorious Reagan, who intended his presidency to end the age of limits in every way excepting his agenda toward corralling the size of government.

Suggestions for Further Reading

1. Lou Cannon, "The Reagan Years," *California Journal*, 5 (Nov. 1974), 360-66.

2. Roger Rapoport, *California Dreaming: The Political Odyssey of Pat and Jerry Brown* (1982).

3. Linda and Theodore Majka, *Farm Workers and the State* (1982).

4. Ronald B. Taylor, *Chavez and the Farm Workers* (1975).

5. Ernesto Galarza, *Farm Workers and Agri-Business in California* (1977).

6. Jack Citrin, *Tax Revolt: Something for Nothing in California* (1982).

7. Terry Schwadron and Paul Richter, eds, *California and the American Tax Revolt: Proposition 13 Five Years Later* (1984).

XIX
THE BOOM OF THE EIGHTIES

California history since 1980 seems more akin to current events than history. Given its temporal proximity, it is difficult to hold the time in any sense of historical perspective. Nonetheless, this narrative continues the story of California's development to the end of the century.

On a most superficial level, this period seems a replay of the last two decades of the nineteenth century. The 1880s was a decade of economic boom and was followed by economic hardship and social upheaval. The 1980s was also a decade of economic boom, followed by hard times and disruption in the following decade. California's economic boom of the 1880s was fueled by transcontinental rail rate cutting. In the 1980s, the boom was encouraged by cheaper energy due to the collapse of the international O.P.E.C. oil cartel early in the decade. But historians should guard against looking only for the similarities between divergent periods. Differences are equally important. For example, governmental fiscal policy on the federal level proved to be a major factor regarding the boom of the 1980s, whereas nothing comparable existed a century before.

Taking office early in 1981, President Ronald Reagan made California's Tax Revolt a national phenomenon. He pushed Congress to cut taxes before undertaking any other business. Winning that battle, he then called for increased military spending in order to check a perceived Soviet superiority in sophisticated weaponry. A wary Congress followed his leadership. These federal policy decisions helped fuel an economic boom across the United States, but the principal beneficiary of his military spending was California, where much of the nation's "military-industrial complex" was housed.

In his Farewell Address of January 17, 1961, President Dwight D. Eisenhower had cautioned his countrymen about the insidious and growing influence of America's "military-industrial complex." During the Reagan presidency, Eisenhower's warning especially had a prophetic ring:

> As we peer into society's future, we—you
> and I, and our government—must avoid the
> impulse to live only for today, plundering,
> for our own ease and convenience, the pre-

cious resources of tomorrow. We cannot
mortgage the material assets of our grand-
children without risking the loss also of their
political and spiritual heritage. We want
democracy to survive for all generations to
come, not to become the insolvent phantom
of tomorrow.

Ronald Reagan built his economic policy decisions upon the
theories of Arthur Laffer, an economist at the University of Southern
California. Laffer had argued that massive tax cuts would fuel a boom
that would produce an increase in federal revenues, thereby easing the
debt problem. But Reagan increased military spending simultaneously with his tax cut and thereby precluded any reliable test of Laffer's theory. Ever since the Great Depression and World War II, the
federal government had carried a substantial debt burden, but until the
late 1970s the nation's public debt had generally grown at a much
slower rate than the overall wealth of the nation. Then, with "stagfla-
tion" (economic stagnation coupled with monetary inflation) during
the presidency of Jimmy Carter, the debt began to show signs of
growing out of proportion to the G.D.P. (Gross Domestic Product).
Ronald Reagan was elected in part to correct this problem. He promised that he could restore prosperity. He did that but at the cost of a
spiraling national debt.
   Unwilling to take responsibility for the worsening debt,
Reagan's Republicans accused Democratic controlled Congresses of
feeding the crisis by their unwillingness to cut federal waste. Democratic social programs were locked into the budget-making process as
"entitlements." Social Security and Medicare/Medicaid grew irrespective of their impact on producing imbalanced annual national budgets.
These facts allowed Republicans to claim that Reaganite fiscal conservatism had been rejected by "tax-and-spend" Democratic congressional majorities. In fact, leaders of both major parties engaged in
fiscal irresponsibility during the decade. As a consequence, the debt
skyrocketed, seemingly out of control. In the short term, there was no
problem. Signs of prosperity could be seen in most parts of American
society. But over time, the mounting debt threatened as a cancer eating at America's economic vitals, feeding off the future well-being of
the nation.

In the short run, a booming economy muted critics. California especially reaped the benefits of national spending for military purposes. As its economy had been geared to the warfare state since World War II, Reagan's investment in "high-tech" weaponry made California's economy the envy of the nation. The monetary fertilizing of California's defense industries also encouraged advances in the state's blossoming electronics industry. New weapons systems were computer driven. California became a design center for Reagan's "Star Wars" (Strategic Defense Initiative) and for advances in avionics designed to guide both combat aircraft and "smart bombs." Military artificial intelligence research pushed the frontiers of technological development. Above and beyond defense spending, advances in both software and hardware characterized a new industry in small personal computers. Much of this innovation occurred in Silicon Valley, a name given to a region stretching southward from Stanford University to San Jose.

In the early nineteenth century, the industrial revolution had been founded upon the mechanized production of cotton textiles. Then, a transportation revolution based on coal, iron and steam-engine technology predominated. This was followed by the age of steel and petroleum. The miracles wrought in Silicon Valley trumpeted yet another stage in an ongoing technological revolution—the age of information. In this new era, the rapid exchange of ideas and exponential developments in technology resulting therefrom (rather than material production per se) commanded center stage. The excellence of California's higher education establishment suggested that the state could long remain a center of this new economic revolution.

In the 1980s, educated technocrats found California to be an intellectual "fast track." New ideas made old modes of production obsolete. The rewards for those on the frontier of these developments were great. By contrast, those with little education, raised in environments placing little value on intellectual prowess, were left farther behind. Throughout the eighties, Californians and Americans at large sensed the widening of a socio-economic division that showed signs of continuing well into the future. During the 1980s, California's dropout rate in public schools broke all previous records. Those lacking the ability to adjust successfully to the skill-intensive shift in modern technology were left with little hope for the future.

American capitalism revealed both its richest treasures and its flotsam and jetsam in California at the close of the century. Home-

Modern California's Population of Mexican Origin or Descent			
Year	Population of Mexican Origin	As % of Hispanics	As % of Total Population
1970	1,856,841	78.4	9.3
1980	3,637,466	80	15.4
1990	6,070,637	80.3	20.4

Most of the Latino population increase in modern California has come from those of Mexican origin. (Data from David E. Lorey, ed., *United States-Mexico Border Statistics Since 1900, 1990 Update*, p. 52).

lessness, drug use and criminal activities multiplied. During the eighties, the state's prison population grew at rates rivaled only by the growth in the national debt. The increasing burden of warehousing prisoners forced state budget planners to cut into public support for education (especially higher education), a wellspring of California's future economic opportunities. Superficially, California in the eighties was a material paradise. Signs of new economic prosperity were evident in new gleaming office buildings and new housing development tracts. But below the surface, something was terribly amiss. San Francisco became a national incubation center of AIDS (Acquired Immune-Deficiency Syndrome) as the deadly new disease spread to threaten the sexual revolution of the sixties. California also became the national leader in teenage pregnancies, which condemned many to lives of dire poverty. By the early 1990s, Los Angeles, San Bernardino and Riverside counties combined had more teen births than the entire state of New York. California's problems were exacerbated by an influx of illegal aliens attracted by the economic boom. Mexico's poverty drove many northward in hopes of a better life. Turmoil in Nicaragua, El Salvador and Guatemala further encouraged a Central American migration of major proportions.

Before the influx of Latinos in the 1980s, Los Angeles had already claimed a large population of Mexican ancestry. By the middle of the eighties, it could be plainly seen that soon "Anglos" might become a minority in California. The birth rate among Latino immigrants far surpassed that of all other groups in the state. Ironically, the Health Rush of the 1880s had swamped historically Latino southern California with "Anglos" from the Midwest. A century later, the tidal forces of demographic growth moved in opposite directions.

Adjusting to the newcomers, California implemented a new state program to serve the needs of "limited English-speaking" students. The federal Civil Rights Act of 1964 had required bilingual education under certain conditions in order to provide "equal opportunity." In 1976, the state legislature installed bilingual/bicultural education in the public schools to allow students to be instructed in their native language while they acquired proficiency in English. The intent was good; the implementation, often nightmarish. While Spanish speakers predominated among the newcomers, over one hundred different languages came to be spoken in the state during the eighties' influx of newcomers from all over the globe. Small school districts could not afford to hire instructors versed in Tagalog, or Haitian Creole or Tahitian. In schools in which most of the students were Spanish speakers, English-speaking African Americans at times were placed in classes taught in Spanish in order to achieve desegregation goals. In addition, for some Spanish-speaking teachers, the goal seemed not so much to wean their students from Spanish but rather to maintain it as a source of cultural pride. As a result, by the end of the decade, the program became controversial. Many students enrolled in it neither acquired an English proficiency nor proved their academic worth. In the 1990s, as the program's promised results were not fulfilled, the California Teachers Association divided bitterly in an internal fight among its members over the issue.

The warning sounds of future social divisions were muffled by a booming economy. Yuppies (young, upwardly mobile professionals) captured the public limelight with their own unique ways of engaging in ostentatious display and conspicuous consumption. Striving to outdo their peers in purchases, these baby-boomers went heavily into personal debt. For the first time, many Californians purchasing a home came to regard three-car garages as a necessity. "Bigger is better" seemed to define the architectural tastes of those buying homes in the eighties.

The decade had begun on a note of extreme fear that the election of hawkish Ronald Reagan might inaugurate World War III and bring nuclear annihilation. As it closed, many continued to behave as if they had no future. Private and public debt skyrocketed as those who had access to borrowing large sums tried to enjoy the present as much as possible. These trends promised a financial time of reckoning in the future.

Slowly at first, and then rapidly, Ronald Reagan's seemingly reckless arms race with the Soviet Union began to bear fruit as indications multiplied that the Soviet Union could not keep pace in Reagan's technological "fast lane." By 1989, the Cold War ended as the Berlin Wall, a symbol of that conflict, came down. Several years later, the Soviet Union itself was no more. Americans rejoiced, but their triumph was tempered by the sobering reality that while their enemy's economic system had gone bankrupt, their own was seemingly on a path toward insolvency. Entering the 1990s, a spiraling national debt demanded immediate attention. Meanwhile, California braced for the predicable impact of reduced defense spending.

Suggestions for Further Reading

1 Randy Shilts, *And the Band Played On: Politics, People, and the AIDS Epidemic* (1987).

2. Michael S. Malone, *The Big Score: The Billion-Dollar Story of Silicon Valley* (1985),

3. Martin Ridge, "Bilingualism, Biculturalism: California's New Past," *Southern California Quarterly*, 66 (Spring 1984), 47-60.

4. Moses Rischin, "Immigration, Migration, and Minorities in California: A Reassessment," *Pacific Historical Review*, 41 (February 1972), 71-90.

5. Sucheng Chan, *Asian Americans* (1991).

XX
CALIFORNIA'S MOOD AT CENTURY'S END

With the Cold War's conclusion, justifications for maintaining California's warfare state became hard to find. As a result, military base closures and termination of defense contracts became the new economic reality. California was harder hit by these changes than any other state. It had benefited most from the Cold War, and it suffered the most at its close. White-collar professionals, as well as blue-collar workers, suddenly found themselves a paycheck away from poverty. Home foreclosures abounded. Middle-aged job seekers, used to high salaries, competed in a job market oriented toward youth. Despair swept many families. The intellectual inventiveness present in the Silicon Valley provided that region with better long-term prospects than southern California, whose economy was locked more into large aircraft production plants. There, the resultant economic downturn revealed the state's worst social problems.

The decline of Los Angeles seemed to define the new decade of the 1990s. Riots, fires and earthquakes, in rapid succession, followed the economic disappointments of vanished defense spending. Los Angeles, which generations before had been termed "the capital of Iowa" due to its Midwestern flavor, was Midwestern no more. Rather, it harbored many diverse cultures and foreign voices—at times screaming at each other. Black/Korean tensions were revealed in the Latasha Harlins case, in which a Korean store clerk shot and killed an African American girl in a confrontation over presumed shoplifting. The shopkeeper received an extremely light punishment from a white judge following a trial monitored closely only in the minority communities involved. Simultaneously, the videotaped beating of Rodney King, a black motorist who had led police on a high-speed chase before being subdued, outraged citizens of all races who could clearly see that excessive force had been used. A subsequent trial of the police officers involved resulted in a verdict generally sympathetic to the excuses of the officers for their extreme behavior. The jury in the case was predominantly white. Immediately following news of the trial's conclusion at the end of April 1992, Los Angeles collapsed into a nearly week-long spasm of anarchic violence.

In the African American community, "uprising" was the term commonly given to the days of rage that came after the King-beating verdict. Elsewhere, "riot" was the preferred terminology. The word choice was significant, for as the decade wore on, blacks and whites often interpreted events from quite different vantage points. While historic black/white animosities captured the headlines during five days of beating, looting and arson, Latinos comprised the largest number of those arrested. Clearly, southern California's growing malaise involved far more ethnic diversity than the traditional black/white racial fissure in American society. At the end of the century, California came to absorb almost half of the immigrant population of the entire nation. By 1990, half of all Angelenos spoke a language other than English in the home; thirty-five percent spoke Spanish. Culturally, Angelenos no longer held much in common.

Despite the fact that California was historically known for its multifaceted anti-Asian heritage, California has become in modern times a favorite new home for immigrants from Asia. Within the decade of the eighties alone, California's Asian/Pacific Islander population almost doubled. It constituted ten percent of the state's population by the time of the Los Angeles upheaval. During the riots, blacks and Latinos commonly vented their rage against successful Korean-American merchants, who suffered disproportionately at the hands of the mobs. Located in south-central Los Angeles, Koreatown received almost no police protection, which typically guarded the more affluent white regions of the city. Despite the efforts of armed storekeepers and friends attempting to protect their properties, Korean stores were looted and gutted. The changing of federal law (primarily the Immigration Act of 1965 dismantling the old ethnically prejudicial quota system in favor of groups maintaining family connections) had encouraged the modern Korean exodus to Los Angeles. Sadly, their suffering in the midst of the rioting underscored the truth that California's long association with anti-Asian prejudice was not entirely a thing of the past.

As images of mayhem were broadcast on the nation's television screens, some compared the event to the sack of Rome by the Vandals in 455. Others justified the widespread thievery by highlighting the larger sums stolen by white-collar looters of savings and loan institutions in the 1980s. The burning of Los Angeles and the rhetoric that followed revealed an ugly underside of American culture that often encourages material well-being by any means necessary. For a century and a half, the golden state had promoted the vaunted "California dream" of a steady progression towards a material paradise. In

April and May of 1992, Los Angeles appeared more as the showcase of a spiritual wasteland.

The initial response of most whites to the rebellion was subdued, as most understood that an injustice had occurred in the trial involving the beating of Rodney King. However, their resentment began to grow as the policemen were found guilty in a second federal trial. Bad feeling came not so much from the conclusion reached but from the perceived certainty of renewed African-American violence if such a verdict were not made. Increasingly, white Angelenos believed that mob rule was replacing democratic governmental processes. This white perception was bolstered by the acquittal of two black men in the "attempted murder" of Reginald Denny, a white truck driver almost beaten to death by a black mob during the Los Angeles upheaval of 1992. Again, the verdict was shrouded by fear that mass violence would ensue if the accused were found guilty of the most serious charges against them.

Nature contributed to southern California's troubles. In October and November 1993, one thousand homes were destroyed in wind-whipped fires over a six-county region. The following January, a devastating earthquake hit both Northridge and the greater Los Angeles area. In the Loma Prieta quake that occurred in the Bay Area during the baseball World Series of 1989, and in a subsequent devastating fire that swept the Oakland hills in 1991, diverse groups had often been brought together in positive ways. But in the Los Angeles quake, the emergency only seemed to increase deepening feelings of resentment between ethnic groups. As many illegal aliens had been dislocated by the Northridge quake, they sought public assistance. Increasingly, citizens began to question why persons who did not belong in the United States should get any public services at all. Indeed, the U.S. Immigration and Naturalization Service estimated that California had almost two million illegal immigrants, forty percent of the national total and almost three times as many as the next highest state. Accordingly, in 1994, California's voters overwhelmingly approved Proposition 187, an initiative barring illegal immigrants from health services, public education and welfare benefits. It was a desperate move. Court challenges quickly tied up the initiative charging that it violated the U.S. Constitution. Nevertheless, Californians again had spoken through their process of "direct democracy." The message they sent was clear. They wanted the federal government to take responsibility for maintaining the national borders, possibly reducing even the rate of legal immigration. In 1996, angry whites outlawed Affirmative Action, passing Proposition 209. In 1998, voters again "sent a message" in passing Proposition 227, which effectively ended California's commitment to bilingual education.

The O.J. Simpson trial of 1995 contributed to the souring mood. Accused of murdering his former wife and her friend Ron Goldman, the former U.S.C. football star created a public spectacle by eluding the law, only to be brought to justice following a televised freeway chase. In a lengthy trial that followed, all participants became overnight celebrities. Daytime soap operas were taken from the airwaves to allow live televised coverage of the more dramatic trial.

A white policeman, who had found key incriminating evidence against Simpson, was proven to be a virulent racist who talked on tape of framing black suspects during his law-enforcement career. A largely African American jury subsequently acquitted the famous black defendant, amidst the tears of the white victims' families. Angry whites emphasized that one bad cop could never have planted all of the evidence against Simpson. A subsequent civil trial, decided by a nearly all-white jury, found Simpson liable for the murders. The lessened standard for guilt in this "wrongful death" suit presumably resulted in the reversal of the earlier verdict. In this latter case, Simpson was theoretically stripped of his wealth. Nonetheless, he remained a free man, a situation that continued to fester in the white mind.

Sensing Los Angeles' decline following the mayhem of 1992, Hollywood film makers produced "Demolition Man," an epic of an ugly, socially divided future Los Angeles governed by veiled force. Professional sports also contributed to the growing malaise. In 1995, Los Angeles lacked a professional football team for the first time since 1946, as both the Rams and the Raiders simultaneously deserted the demoralized city. By the mid-nineties, many if not most southern Californians believed that their state had already experienced its best days. Many feared declining economic opportunities, as existing business enterprises escaped to states with lower taxes, lower wages, more affordable housing and fewer governmental regulations. Debt-strapped or bankrupt city and county governments, drive-by shootings and an increasing number of gated communities seemed to characterize the emerging development of an undesirable California.

One hundred years before, a similar pessimism clouded the public mood. Articulated then by Frederick Jackson Turner, it suggested that the wellsprings of economic opportunity for the common person had all but disappeared. Yet this later proved not to be the case. Recollection of this earlier misjudgment encourages hope. Indeed, many positive signs brighten modern California's horizon. These deserve some attention at the close of this history. For one, the persistent smog problem of southern California appears to be coming under control. Since 1979, the number of stage-one smog alerts in the Los Angeles basin has steadily declined. Second, a workable plan to manage water resources, a perennial problem for southern California, also seems to be materializing. No one envisions huge new water projects being built. Rather, hope lies in better management of existing resources, with cities purchasing water from marginal farmers as one key ingredient in the overall process. Unfortunately, this bright spot results from a major negative development. As California farming is typically irrigated agriculture, California soils are susceptible to salinization problems over long periods of continued use. While twenty-five percent of all table food produced in the United States is currently grown in California, agricultural operations will inevitably be reduced by soil salinization. Accordingly, few observers expect California agriculture to dominate in the state's future economy as it has in the past. California's cities will reap the benefit in available water supplies.

A third optimistic sign stems from the fact that many California immigrants and their children are familiar with Asian cultures and languages. This promises to make California a contender for dominating the future commerce of the Pacific Rim. The North American Free Trade Agreement (NAFTA) also holds special opportunities for California with its large Spanish-speaking population. In 1995, San Jose (Silicon Valley) and Los Angeles-Long Beach held the positions of third and fourth, respectively, for dollar value of exports from American urban centers, trailing only Detroit and New York City. Twenty-five percent of the nation's international trade comes through California. Prospects are likely that this share will continue to grow.

The state continues to be responsible for one-eighth of America's economic output. Thirty-two of America's hundred fastest-growing business enterprises are in California. In 1997, California's output of goods and services exceeded $1 trillion dollars for the first time. The state's economic product is just ahead of China, greater than all of Eastern Europe and the Middle East, equal to that of the entire South American continent, double that of both Africa and the

Russian Federation. If California were a separate nation, it would rank seventh in the world economically, just behind Great Britain in productive capacity. In short, while modern California's problems are real, so are its opportunities. Indeed, by 1996, pundits again were proclaiming California's latest economic resurrection. Foreign trade, high-tech exports, entertainment products and tourism were credited with the rebound, which in that year produced $2.6 billion dollars more in tax revenues for the annual state budget than had been anticipated.

In Silicon Valley, the boom has been especially noticeable. There, entrepreneurial opportunities have outstripped the availability of high-tech labor. Indeed, as of 1997, forty percent of the research and development jobs in the valley were filled by immigrants, revealing a high dependency upon foreign talent. Increasingly, this factor together with the lower labor costs in former Third World countries is encouraging high-tech California firms to locate their research and development shops in foreign countries. With faster and more reliable networking technology, such foreign sites do not hamper productivity as might have been the case even as recently as the 1980s. Consequently, the global tentacles of Silicon Valley reveal one key aspect of California's future economy.

California's future will be closely integrated with that of the entire planet. In one sense, this is a new development. Yet, throughout all of its history, California has never been isolated. In this volume, California has been described as having long been in a continuous relationship with both the rest of the nation and the world. Irrespective of what the earliest European explorers thought of California's geography, the region has in fact never been an island. California has long served as a beacon toward a better life, popularly termed the "California Dream." The first Spanish explorers of the land estimated it to be located close to paradise. Indeed, they gave it the name "California" for that very reason. Much later, the Gold Rush added a special glitter to this mythological reputation. Some came and struck it rich. Others discovered only dashed hopes. In March 1997, thirty nine persons belonging to a small collective known as Heaven's Gate committed mass suicide in Rancho Santa Fe, a posh suburb of San Diego. Most of them carried out-of-state driver's licenses. Californians only in their choice of the state as their ultimate earthly destination, they were part of a religious cult believing that their suicides would lead to a "physical kingdom level above human."

Why did they choose California as the launching pad for
their departure from this mortal coil? Indeed, why had Jim Jones a
generation before brought his Peoples Temple from Indiana to San
Francisco seeking spiritual and physical liberation before finding
mass suicide in a Guyanese jungle? Why did Charles Manson, a son
of Cincinnati, come to California to find his twisted version of nir-
vana? As a place of few traditions, California beckons risk takers and
innovators seeking paths that are commonly neither tolerated nor encouraged in their locations of origin. The inventiveness of California,
which will certainly continue into the twenty-first century, will include new technological wonders, spawned in places such as Silicon
Valley; unfortunately, it will also include the stories of others who
come seeking the end of the rainbow only to find an empty pot. But
whatever their individual destinies, Californians will likely remain a
people drawn from the world over and defined more by their fantastic
quests than their varied origins—a people of high expectations seeking visions unimaginable elsewhere.

Suggestions for Further Reading

1. John M. Allswang, "Tom Bradley of Los Angeles,"
Southern California Quarterly, 74 (Spring 1992), 55-105.
2. Mark Baldassare, *The Los Angeles Riots: Lessons for the
Urban Future* (1994).
3. Sonia Maasik and Jack Solomon, *California Dreams and
Realities, Readings for Critical Thinkers and Writers* (1995).
4. Alvin and Heidi Toffler, Brian Cross, *It's Not About A
Salary—Rap, Race, and Resistance in Los Angeles* (1993).
5. Marc Reisner, *Cadillac Desert: The American West and
Its Disappearing Water* (1986).
6. Mike Davis, *City of Quartz, Excavating the Future in Los
Angeles* (1990).
7. Paul M. Ong, *et al.*, eds., *The New Asian Immigration in
Los Angeles and Global Restructuring* (1994).
8. Timothy P. Fong, *The First Suburban Chinatown: The
Remaking of Monterey Park, California* (1994).
9. John Horton, *The Politics of Diversity: Immigration, Resistance, and Change in Monterey Park, California* (1995).

General Index

Author Index

Index

www.ingramcontent.com/pod-product-compliance
Lightning Source LLC
Chambersburg PA
CBHW031252090426
42742CB00007B/423